Emotional Intelligence

Change your thinking
get more from your life

Karen Kircher

First published 2022 by Malcolm Down Publishing Ltd.
www.malcolmdown.co.uk

24 23 22 22   7 6 5 4 3 2 1

British Library Cataloguing in Publication Data
A catalogue record for this book is available from the British Library.

ISBN 978-1-915046-21-5

Cover design and illustrations by Adam Jenkins
www.adamjenkins.design

Printed in the UK

Commendations

—

This book provides a highly accessible journey into a topic often written about in language that is far too academic. It lays out in a practical way how best to understand emotions, explains how they can get the better of you, and provides simple tools to develop yourself and better appreciate those around you. Surely compulsory reading for young and old alike.

Phil Brown , Executive Coach at Hurren Brown, formerly Head of People Development at Anglian Water

Karen has managed to distil many years of experience as a coach of a wide range of people, in business, public and voluntary sector bodies, into this invaluable guide. The reader who is interested in understanding, grappling with and turning to advantage their emotional intelligence will find much to learn and apply from this practical workbook.

Professor Clive Morton OBE, Ph. D, CCIPD, CEng, MICE

For over 25 years Karen has been working with individuals and teams from all walks of life teaching them how to obtain and maintain fuller more rewarding relationships. Karen's clear and detailed explanation of EI, frequently reviewing my Priorities and considering my Belief Tree, helped me understand what makes me tick and, most importantly, how I could behave more positively. These tools enabled me to change my behaviours and my reactions, resulting in healthier relationships with family, friends and colleagues. Karen's book now enables a much wider audience to learn and practise these skills, thus change their lives and enjoying happier relationships – thank you Karen for sharing these life-changing gifts.

Jackie Fox, Group Company Secretary, CCLA

Acknowledgements

—

I wish to thank Professor Clive Morton, who introduced me to the subject of emotional intelligence through the late Anita Hall and has acted as mentor and encourager to me personally for over twenty-five years. Clive leads by example in so much that is contained in the contents of this book and I thank him for the wisdom and support he has shown me.

I also wish to thank the many clients who have been a part of my career as we explored the subject of emotional intelligence together. It has been an absolute privilege to work with each of you. I cherish those light bulb moments as things fall into place and your stories of success as you have learnt to live a more fulfilled life alongside leading and influencing others effectively in the workplace. There are few that can say they get paid for having fun and I am one of the lucky ones!

Contents

—

Part 3

Emotional intelligence and how you communicate, influence and lead

Introduction: Why this book?
—

Over the years I have had the pleasure of coaching hundreds of people working in business, healthcare, education, central and local government, and the voluntary sector. Although coaching is tailored, one subject consistently crops up: emotional intelligence.

Whether running the gauntlet of corporate life or managing a family, classroom or hospital ward, being able to read your own and other people's emotional signals and react appropriately can make such a difference. Life is about relationships, which explains why so many people seek to understand their emotional intelligence. They may desire greater confidence and self-belief in order to deal with fears and anxieties that hold them back. The majority simply want to understand what makes themselves and others tick by recognising their own and others' emotions and how to manage emotional responses accordingly. Like words running through a stick of rock, getting to grips with your emotional intelligence is core to how you build stronger relationships and so effectively communicate, influence and lead others.

This book has evolved alongside those people I have been privileged to coach. Every time we turn the pages together, I also get to discover more about my own emotional intelligence. Understanding and developing it is rather like peeling an onion. You start with the outer

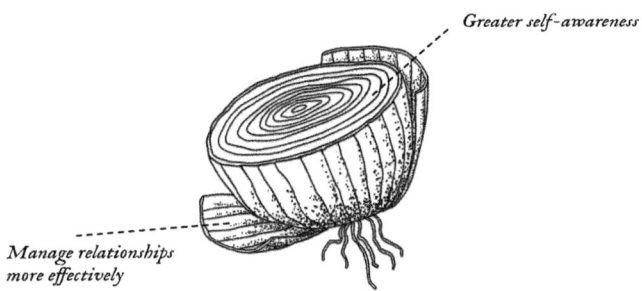

Greater self-awareness

Manage relationships more effectively

9

layer, which provides greater self-awareness. As you peel further layers you gain an even deeper understanding of managing relationships more effectively, both with your self and others. Peeling layers as you go, this book is not a 'quick fix' solution to understanding your emotional intelligence – developing it does not work that way. Instead, it is like a guidebook, helping you navigate a journey that will evolve over many years. You will no doubt do an initial read through, which I hope you find invaluable. However, more aspects of your emotional intelligence will become apparent each time you browse through the contents. As the pages become well-worn you will gain greater insight into not only your emotional intelligence but also that of those you encounter and lead daily.

Significantly, understanding your emotional intelligence is an essential component of being an effective leader in the sense that: **leadership is not just for those with a formal title, position, or authority.** Whoever you are and whatever your role in society, you have opportunities to demonstrate good leadership every day with those you encounter, however small those moments may be. Such a definition of leadership applies at any level and across all walks of life whatever the 'work': salaried, volunteering, in the home raising a family or other day-to-day connections. This is about leading positively in those contexts. We can all be significant as leaders, though some do go on to have more prominent, formal leadership roles.

I do not describe myself as an academic or subject matter expert, just someone with a love of people who has always been interested in why they behave the way they do. As I have explored my own emotional intelligence, I have come to recognise how important it is for everyone to have the opportunity to understand and manage it. I believe you can overcome any limiting thoughts you have believed about yourself and others. These negative thoughts hold you back and restrict your ability to connect with those around you, restrict your ability to reach your full potential, affect your well-being and stop you experiencing the fullness of life itself. By shifting such inner thoughts and emotional responses you can start to enjoy the freedom to be 'you' without the need for approval from, or comparison with, others.

Book contents

Part 1 explains emotional intelligence, exploring how your belief system is created, your 'sensitive spots' and the impact of experiences and Golden Rules learnt in your formative years.

Part 2 teaches you how to defuse any 'trigger' situation by changing your internal narrative (because that impacts the way you see yourself and the world around you). Shifting your inner thought pattern enables you to experience the fullness of life available to you whether at work or in your personal relationships. It also tackles the impact of busyness and how to build personal resilience and greater balance into your life. As you learn to manage your emotional intelligence and keep yourself 'in balance' you are less likely to react negatively.

Part 3 combines what you have learnt with practical topics such as how to handle conflict, your ability to communicate with and influence others, and how to become the leader you yourself would choose to follow. Bringing these elements together will enhance your ability to build stronger, heathier, trusting relationships.

As you work through the material take time to reflect on what you are learning and complete the activities. It may help to pause before carrying on to the next chapter and by doing this you will get the most from this book. I also encourage you to make a contract with yourself to complete the book, paying particular attention to the earlier chapters, because then the outcomes from parts two and three will be richer. As you change your thinking and perspective on how you see yourself and how you believe others will respond to you, I believe you will discover greater joy and contentment.

Be Aware

Some of the content of this book will require you to deep dive into the past and, for this reason, I encourage you to identify one or two close friends/family who you might like to talk things through with as they arise. This is not meant to alarm you, just a gentle warning that 'stuff' can surface that it is important to process alongside having fun exploring your emotional intelligance to discover who you truly are. As you work through the chapters, you will begin to recognise what has held you back and more importantly what to do to move forward.

You may have a belief system that has been influenced by serious physical or emotional trauma experienced in childhood which has left deep scars. If you recognise you have been seriously broken by events in life, take a step of courage and find a trusted friend and/or specialist therapist or psychologist who will be able to help you overcome your internal thoughts. This may or may not be the book for you, but certainly you will need a support network before reading some of the content.

Understand your emotional intelligence

—

Chapter 1. What we mean by emotional intelligence
—

Before we go any further let us clarify the differences between intellectual intelligence, emotional intelligence and personality traits, all of which make you uniquely who you are.

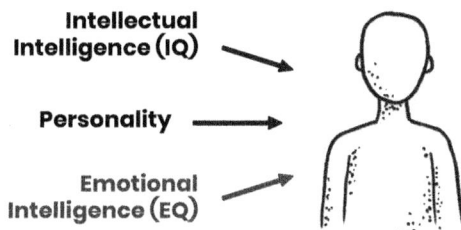

Intellectual and emotional intelligence are distinct qualities that determine how you think and act.

Intellectual intelligence is the understanding of facts and concepts together with your ability to reason, plan, solve problems, think objectively, comprehend ideas and learn from experience. It is responsible for processing information, reasoning, knowing and operating your working memory.

Emotional intelligence is the capacity to be aware of, control and express one's emotions. It taps into a fundamental element of human behaviour that is distinct from the intellect and is used to handle interpersonal relationships judiciously and empathetically. Emotional intelligence cannot be predicted based on IQ: you may have a high IQ but your EQ could be low.

Personality is the collection of characteristics and qualities that distinguish an individual from others. To understand these personality traits it can be helpful to explore what is known as the 'Big Five Model' or 'OCEAN Model'[1], which identifies five significant characteristics of personality:

1. Openness to experience: How inventive and curious you are vs how consistent and cautious.
2. Conscientiousness: How efficient and organised you are vs how extravagant and careless.
3. Extroversion: How outgoing and energetic you are vs how solitary and reserved (i.e. introversion).
4. Agreeableness: How friendly and compassionate you are vs how critical and rational.
5. Neuroticism: How sensitive and nervous you are vs how resilient and confident.

Personality traits are not directly related to EQ and IQ (high or low). The combination of your IQ, EQ and personality makes you unique in terms of who you are.

Having established the differences between these three, let us now focus our attention specifically on emotional intelligence. It is worth noting that it is often referred to by different terminology as highlighted in the following definition:

> Emotional intelligence (EI), emotional quotient (EQ) and emotional intelligence quotient (EIQ), is the capability of individuals to recognise their own emotions and those of others, discern between different feelings and label them appropriately, use emotional information to guide thinking and behaviour and adjust emotions to adapt to environments.[2]

Emotional intelligence comprises two key skills: personal and social competence.

| **1. Personal competence** | ⟶ | **Self-awareness** | ⟶ | **Self-management** |
| **2. Social competence** | ⟶ | **Social awareness** | ⟶ | **Relationship management** |

Personal competence focuses on you as an individual and is divided into self-awareness and self-management. Social competence looks at how you behave with other people and is divided into social awareness and relationship management. You must first travel the personal competence journey to understand your own emotional intelligence and adjust your EQ accordingly. Such adjustments enable you to objectively read social situations without 'your stuff' getting in the way thereby developing your social competence. Such emotional maturity enables you to manage all relationships effectively and with empathy. The following quote perfectly captures this journey: 'Human beings, by changing the inner attitudes of their minds, can change the outer aspects of their lives.'[3]

Whether you realise it or not, your emotional intelligence impacts you and those around you (daily!) Emotional intelligence is about managing 'The Gap': that split second, between something happening (a trigger/ stimulus) and a reaction (your response).

From the moment you get up to the time you go to bed 'things' happen around you that stimulate an automatic, usually subconscious, response. It may be a child not getting ready for school, a late train, an aggressive email from a colleague, a difficult conversation with a customer, a manager assigning you a task you have no time or experience to complete, something funny said by a toddler that makes you laugh, a friend who has ignored your call or text message – the list is endless! When something happens (a trigger) it begins the physical pathway for your emotional intelligence by activating your primary senses. To think rationally about the experience (trigger) your primary senses must travel to the front of your brain, which requires them to travel through the limbic system, the place where emotional responses are experienced. Emotional intelligence requires effective communication between the emotional and rational centres of the brain.

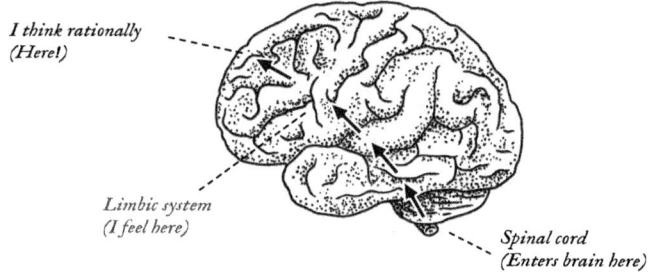

I think rationally (Here!)

Limbic system (I feel here)

Spinal cord (Enters brain here)

Billions of microscopic neurons along this pathway enable information to travel between the rational and emotional centres. Rather like a favourite walk, regularly navigating this pathway enables the information to travel freely strengthening the connection between the rational and emotional centres of the brain. The pathway becomes easier to navigate as you consider what you are thinking and feeling and then doing something productive with those thoughts and feelings. We spend much of the time ignoring our thoughts and feelings or even getting run over by them! Most lapses in emotional intelligence come from a simple lack of awareness and understanding.

Healthy, strong relationships require us to manage our emotions, which are very much a part of us. Learning how to manage them in the best way can make a real difference in how we interact with others. Emotions do not stay at home just because we head to work. We are human beings not human doings, impacted by how we feel whether we acknowledge this or not. Emotions can steer us in many directions, affecting our mood, tone and behaviour. Because many of us are taught from childhood that some emotions are bad, we invest considerable time trying to ignore them in the hope that they will just go away – they don't! They simply hang around like annoying back-seat drivers, blocking our ability to build and maintain good relationships.

If we allow it, our internal narrative (like the voice of a chatterbox) will transmit negative thoughts about self and the people around us. Such thoughts impact on our expectations, govern our behaviour and lead us to view experiences in a way that reinforces those negative thoughts. They become a repetitive loop playing in our thinking and when left unchecked become constraints, choking the fulfilling life available to us. The sooner we become aware of our thoughts and emotions and recognise how they impact on us, the sooner we will be able to stop them negatively controlling our life. Understanding and managing The Gap is the only way to get the most from each day, enabling us to achieve both our career and personal goals.

Did you know you can experience around 25 emotions each waking hour? With roughly 16 waking hours each day, this means you can potentially have 400 emotional experiences per day, 2,800 per week and more than 145,000 per year! Of all the emotions you will experience in your lifetime, a significant proportion will happen during working hours. This helps us to understand why people who manage emotions effectively are easier to work with and more likely to achieve what they set out to deliver.

Take a few minutes to complete the following activity to explore the impact your thoughts and emotions have on your life. There are no right or wrong answers but it is important to be honest with yourself.

Activity: My thoughts and emotions

To what extent do my emotional responses control the way I live my life? Score between 1: 'They totally control me' and 10 'I understand and manage them effectively'.

1   2   3   4   5   6   7   8   9   10

Why I gave myself this score:

Am I aware of: 1 My internal narrative (thoughts)? 2 My emotions and how I am feeling? 3 Both my thoughts and emotions? 4 Neither?

What would I like to change in terms of my emotional responses and and the impact they have on my life?

Chapter 2. How your belief system is created

—

To understand how your internal voice has taken up residence, let us start at the beginning by looking at how our belief system is created. From the moment we are conceived we start to gather information: what we see, hear, sense, feel, smell, what happens to us and what is said to us are all stored in our belief system and contribute to how it develops. Whether from parents, other formative adults or from the events we are witnessing, we take such experiences personally and make positive and negative decisions about ourselves and the world around us.

It is interesting that identical twins raised together, experiencing almost identical situations over their first few years, will have belief systems that develop differently. This is because we absorb information as both actual and perceived. Try asking one of your siblings about a shared early childhood memory and you will each probably recall it differently, based on your individual perceptions.

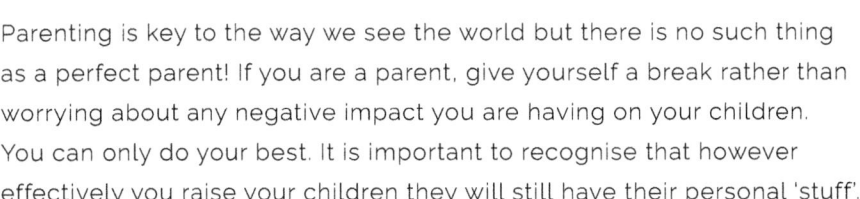

Parenting is key to the way we see the world but there is no such thing as a perfect parent! If you are a parent, give yourself a break rather than worrying about any negative impact you are having on your children. You can only do your best. It is important to recognise that however effectively you raise your children they will still have their personal 'stuff'.

Around the age of two we become more mobile and our world enlarges, giving us many opportunities to explore and interact with others. We continue to absorb positive feedback but also disapproval. By the age of five a child could have heard the word 'No' 50,000 times. Responsible adults must use the word 'No' to teach children good values and behaviours, and keep them safe but a child often picks up the non-verbal energy of the 'No' rather than the verbal message. Having been there myself with my three children I recognise that when I was tired, stressed and out of balance what they heard and saw may not have been as positive as I had hoped!

By seven we have sorted and re-filed all the evidence, adding labels to the files on our 'memory stick'. From the evidence stored and because we have become more self-conscious, we start judging and comparing ourself against our siblings and other children: 'prettier?', 'cleverer?', 'a faster runner?', 'more popular?', 'loved more than me?' (the comparison game). Such thought patterns reinforce any positive and negative decisions previously made about ourselves. The foundations of our belief system are firmly in place and we spend the rest of our lives looking for evidence that reinforces we are right!

At puberty, the effect of hormones rushing through the body affects self-esteem and self-confidence, which are either enhanced or subdued. We continue collecting evidence that we are right about our beliefs, solidifying such thoughts. By the time we reach adulthood we have created our own custom-made, belief system that directly affects the way we see ourselves and the world around us. How you perceive and react to the world is driven from your unique belief system.

Sensitive spots are markers in your belief system, where you are particularly convinced to the extent that your behaviour is heavily influenced by your thoughts, beliefs, emotions, memories, etc. If a trigger activates a 'sensitive spot', which you are not consciously controlling, this prompts you to feel, react and perform in certain ways that is on display for others to pick up. Similarly, other people are prompted to react and all the responses collide either in harmony or discord with each other, creating the 'mood music' in the room. As adults, what we sense (see, hear, feel) can have little to do with the current issue, but is a combination of each person's emotional experiences from the past.

Your thoughts, beliefs, emotions and memories can help you to achieve and do your best, but they can also cause you to hold back, create stress or lead to inadvertent reaction to those around you. Your responses can put you on a collision course with other people and even yourself and can cause you more problems than you had to begin with. Once you recognise your sensitive spots, you can work to minimise their negative impact on your actions by rewiring your brain to think differently in reaction to triggers.

Chapter 3. Understanding 'The Gap'

—

The transition in how you feel between experiencing a trigger and your response is The Gap, where your thoughts, beliefs, memories and emotions are prompted into creating a reaction.

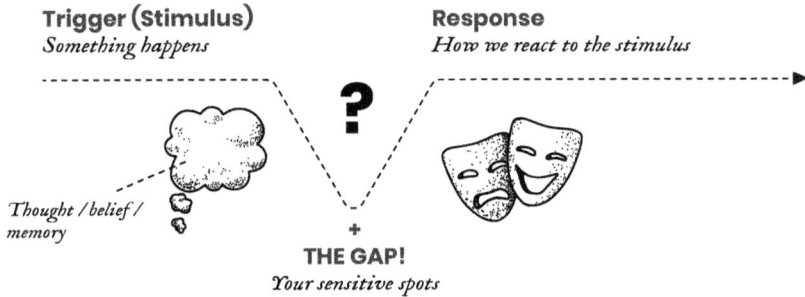

Trigger (Stimulus)
Something happens

Response
How we react to the stimulus

Thought / belief / memory

?

+
THE GAP!
Your sensitive spots

Each thought, belief and/or memory can be positive or negative, for example 'Is anyone listening to me?', 'No one cares, people always ignore me.' The emotions experienced can be an array of feelings, that run through our bodies throughout the day, interacting with each other and the amount of emotion attached determines their impact. It can be like dominoes or bowling pins, once one is triggered others follow. Some cultures do not approve of emotional displays or being emotional, so from an early age we may learn to suppress our emotions. However, because 93% of communication between people in conversation is non-verbal, **your emotions are on display 24 hours a day whether you are aware of this or not.** You pick up moods of your colleagues, family and friends even when they say nothing. For example, it might be a facial gesture or simply 'that glare' you give that shows your disapproval as you make eye contact. The overflow of emotions and out-of-control emotional reactions are at the root of many conflicts and upsets. Emotions hold your belief system and sensitive spots in place and the amount of emotion connected determines the magnitude of your potential reaction.

We are all brought up differently when it comes to expressing our emotions. Some are taught to let it all out, even if it means hurting others. Many are told that expressing emotion is bad. Boys are often shamed when they cry because it shows weakness, girls are sometimes told off for not being ladylike when in a rage and most children are at some point told to calm down when they are too excited. What we fail to recognise is that our emotions are completely natural but that how we express them can have a positive or negative impact. Emotions are an important part of your personal energy but when they become trapped as you store them up, rather than safely discharging them, they can be released uncontrollably and with potentially devastating results. If your emotions remain trapped inside they can have a detrimental effect on both your mental and physical well-being.

Emotions

Whilst the experience and expression of emotions such as joy and love have that feel-good factor, all emotions are important and have a role in helping us express how we are feeling. It is important not to limit our emotional vocabulary by separating our emotions into 'acceptable' and 'unacceptable'. Instead, learn to acknowledge the full range of emotions and how to manage all of them effectively. They all connect with our internal thoughts, beliefs and memories and can be categorised as joy, love, anger, disgust, sadness, fear, panic, guilt, and shame.

Of all the different emotions, **Joy** is one that people strive for the most. Joy is a pleasant emotional state that is characterised by feelings of contentment, happiness, gratification, satisfaction and well-being. It is an emotional response that typically arises when something positive has happened to us or someone important to us, or when our needs are met. The feeling of joy helps us to know what is important to us and makes us seek more of it. Joy connects us to our core identity, values and priorities and is the emotion that makes life worth living in the moment. It is not just based on whether things are going well or not because it can remain even amidst any suffering. Joy is an emotion that's acquired by the anticipation, acquisition or even the expectation of something great and wonderful.

To feel the emotion of **Love** is to have an intense feeling of deep affection and concern toward another person or a great interest and pleasure in something. Our mind triggers the emotion of love to motivate us to move closer to people or things that have the potential to make us happy. To truly experience love is to operate from a place of complete unconditional acceptance, allowing someone to be exactly as they are (including one's self), without any belief that they are not good enough or could be 'better' if they were different. It is selfless, with no requirement for anything in return because there is nothing it needs. It is important to recognise people's attributes do not stop us loving them, judging them does that! When, instead of love we feel anger, disappointment or resentment, or just feel isolated from someone, that can prevent us from loving them and that includes ourselves.

Many of us do not like to admit when we feel **Anger** because of what we have been taught about it in childhood. Instead, we use words that sound more palatable, such as feeling frustrated, annoyed or irritated but all of these are different expressions of anger. It is important to recognise the emotion of anger and learn how to feel and process it, but more on this later.

Disgust arises as a feeling of aversion towards something we perceive as offensive. We can feel disgusted by something we perceive with our physical senses (see, hear, smell, touch, taste), by the actions or appearances of people and even by ideas. Disgust may also alternate with the feeling of anger if the disgusted person is angry about being made to feel disgust. Disgust is easily expressed by facial expression, vocal expression and physical sensations.

Sadness is a powerful emotion characterised by loss, grief, sorrow, hurt, disconnection or being let down. Again, it is important to acknowledge when we feel sad and learn how to express it safely.

Fear arises with the threat of harm, either physical, emotional, or psychological, real or imagined. While traditionally considered a 'negative' emotion, fear serves an important role in keeping us safe as it mobilises us to cope with potential danger. The emotion of fear is often associated with the fear of failure, the fear of rejection (being alone) and the fear of unpredictability. All three can have a crippling effect because they have the potential to stop us in our tracks or make us respond out of character.

Panic is a sudden sensation of fear, which is so strong it can dominate or prevent reason and logical thinking, replacing it with an overwhelming feeling of anxiety and frantic agitation. This makes us react with fight or flight behaviour (i.e. resist forcibly or run away).

The final two emotions need clarification because they can get mistaken for each other. **Guilt** is about feeling guilty for something you have done, for example 'I feel guilty about how I spoke aggressively to my partner.' Guilt goes against the values and beliefs you have been raised with; you feel it when you know you are in the wrong. **Shame** goes much deeper because it is about how you see yourself and begins with an 'I am ...' learnt from childhood or through trauma. For example, when you were young, if you had older siblings constantly telling you that you were a nuisance, this could have created shame i.e. 'I am a nuisance.' As an adult you may struggle to ask for help because you do not want to be a nuisance. Other examples are: 'I am ugly', 'I am stupid', 'I am unworthy', 'I am unwanted'. If you have experienced any physical or emotional trauma, or neglect these can easily be associated with shame.

Prompts

Now we have identified the main array of emotions you can experience any day, let us start to explore the thoughts and beliefs at the root of your sensitive spots, more generally referred to as **emotional Prompts.** Prompts can be broken down into 'Parent Rule Prompts' and 'Child Feeling Prompts'.

1.   **Parent Rule Prompts** are the parental, inner-critic thoughts and beliefs about yourself and others. They cover all sorts of harsh, negative or unrealistic words or phrases, which you say to yourself in a tone and manner that is judgemental, demanding or nasty. These are learnt, directly or indirectly, from your earlier experiences. They might sound like this: 'I'm not good enough, I'm so stupid I always make mistakes, I'm responsible for other people's happiness.' Such Prompts have woven themselves into the fabric of your belief system, which is why you do not tend to question them – because by adulthood, they are a fundamental part of your identity.

2.   **Child Feeling Prompts** are representations of the self which came into being in childhood in response to the parenting you received and other experiences you encountered. Such Prompts are where your unmet needs as a child reside e.g. wanting understanding and connection. Child Feeling Prompts tend to get stuck in the past, with only an awareness of what happened back then. Whilst there is the 'Contented Child' who feels loved, contented, connected, satisfied, fulfilled, protected, accepted, praised, there are other Child Feeling Prompts that can negatively impact on your thoughts and behaviour. The 'Vulnerable Child' feels lonely, isolated, sad, misunderstood, unsupported, defective, deprived, and responds from such hurts. The 'Angry Child' feels intensely angry, enraged, infuriated, frustrated, impatient because their want is to get a need met but they go about it in an unhelpful way, having a potentially destructive impact on relationships. The 'Undisciplined Child' acts on desires or impulses in a selfish or uncontrolled way, developed either from a lack of discipline

during childhood (i.e. giving in to the child and poor limit setting) or the opposite whereby the childhood environment was very stern, rigid and strict with harsh discipline. Such Child Feeling Prompts affect your ability to regulate yourself and your emotions in a healthy adult way.

Think about the negative messaging your inner narrative transmits to you and the types of Prompt it helps to create. It may be around being not good enough/stupid/a failure? Maybe about being disregarded/ unsupported/unworthy? Perhaps controlled/powerless/weak or related to duty/loyalty/feeling responsible? Of course, each time you go through this book other Prompts may occur to you. It took me five years to recognise two of my biggest emotional Prompts (Be Perfect, Be Strong), both of which often activate alongside 'Responsible'. The role of parent can be (very) challenging and the purpose of this exercise is simply to be real with what you have experienced or perceived, whilst remaining respectful to parents and figures of authority from childhood.

Activity: Identifying my emotional Prompts

Read through the following list and tick those that you can relate to and these will be a good place to start.

You can revisit this list and update it as often as you wish.

Prompts (Parent Rule)	Tick	Prompts (Child Feeling)	Tick
Authority		Abandoned	
Be Perfect		Alone	
Be Strong		Betrayed	
Better Than		Commitment	
Committed		Controlled	
Controlling		Disregarded	
Critical		Disrespected	
Duty		Failure	
Equality		Impatient (faster/better)	

Prompts (Parent Rule)	Tick	Prompts (Child Feeling)	Tick
Failure		Less Than	
Impatient (Get on with it)		Loss	
Intolerant		Not Good Enough	
Injustice		Out of Control	
Irresponsible		Powerless	
Less Than		Public Embarrassment	
Loyalty		Rejection/Rejected	
Manners		Stupid	
Money		Ugly	
Not Good Enough		Undeserving	
Rebel		Unimportant	
Respect		Unlovable	
Responsible		Unsafe	
Trust		Unsupported	
Wrong		Unwanted	
		Unworthy	
		Valueless	
		Victim	
		Weak	
		Worry	
		Wrong	

You may identify a thought pattern that feels different to the Prompts listed, which is just as important to capture. Use your own word(s) to describe such thoughts, e.g. 'Invisible'.

Prompt	Tick

Begin to recognise when you feel 'activated', i.e. your negative thoughts and/or emotion(s) have had a fuse lit. Take time to review the list and ask yourself, 'Which Prompt(s) have gone off?' Take a photo of the list so you can quickly reference it wherever you are, rather than trying to remember how you felt subsequently. Record your observations and do this as often as you can.

Levels of competence

Now you have begun to explore your Prompts you will have a heightened awareness of when you do not handle situations effectively. You may not, however, be able to correct your response. At this stage simply celebrate you have recognised a Prompt has been activated – that is a good start!

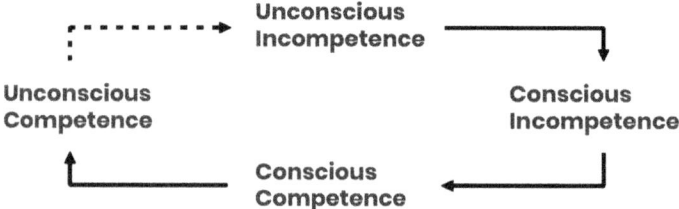

Getting to grips with your emotional intelligence is like learning to ride a bike. Initially you have no awareness you are unable to ride (unconsciousness incompetence). When you sit on the saddle you are faced with your reality (conscious incompetence). You work hard to learn, at first wobbling and occasionally falling off but gradually, with much effort and concentration, you begin to co-ordinate everything (conscious competence). You eventually reach the moment when you are cycling along without having to think about how to ride (unconscious competence)[4]. Recognise when you have just entered the conscious incompetence phase of understanding your emotional intelligence and do not be too hard on yourself. You will wobble and at times make mistakes but by persevering you will begin to master it. However, as you begin to combat and reconcile certain Prompts, others may surface and you will go through the stages of the competence cycle again.

Over the coming weeks, consider which Prompts are regularly activating, which act in combination and which have greatest impact. Add further ticks against a Prompt (in the previous activity) when you know it has manifested itself so that over time you begin to see patterns. Do not feel you have to rush the process; you might like to pause at this stage simply to explore your Prompts before reading on. When you feel you have identified some patterns, complete the following activity.

Activity: Prompt rating

Record the Prompts you have identified and whether you believe them to be small, medium, or large (by how many ticks each have accrued). Think about which Prompts tend to activate together e.g. Not Good Enough and Stupid.

Prompts I relate to	Small	Medium	Large
1			
2			
3			
4			
5			
6			
7			
8			
9			
10			
11			
12			

Chapter 4. How 'The Gap' affects your life
—

What is stored in The Gap affects your state of mind and how you feel about yourself and the world around you every day. When you find yourself feeling stressed and anxious this is often a result of how you are using your emotional intelligence. As you become more aware of it and learn to work with it, the more you can alleviate the stress and tension in your life, reducing the risk of major physical and mental illnesses.

Identifying a Prompt has been triggered is one of the most challenging aspects of working with these concepts and it can be helpful to recognise how certain behaviours link to your Prompts.

Activity: How I react to my Prompts

Read through the list below to identify familiar thoughts and behaviours. Tick those you recognise and consider how they relate to the Prompts you have identified. This provides a link between your Prompts and your internal thinking and associated behavioural responses.

Thoughts and behaviours	Tick	Related Prompt(s)
Comparing myself to others: feeling inferior (less than) or superior (more than)		
Judging myself and others (over-critical)		
Inability to give to myself by participating fully		
Feeling/acting/talking negatively or like a victim		

Thoughts and behaviours	Tick	Related Prompt(s)
Over-allow (sacrifice) putting others' wants, needs and desires before mine		
Big fish in a small pond – staying in my comfort zone		
Saying 'I can't'		
Saying 'I should' often		
Breaking agreements often		
Lying/not telling the truth		
Spending time with people who feel/act/ talk negatively		
Rejecting people who love me		
Unable to say how I feel		
Getting disproportionately angry for a 'crime' committed/no obvious reason		
Watch a lot of TV (or other distractions) as a way of not dealing with how I feel		
Poor personal hygiene and lack of self-care		
Not taking holidays		

Activity: The links between Prompts, thinking and behaviour

Bring together what you have learnt about your emotional intelligence by identifying two recent situations when you recognise a reaction was triggered. What were your thoughts and behaviours and which Prompt(s) were involved?

Situation 1

What happened (the trigger)?

What did I think and how did I behave?

Which Prompt(s) activated?

Situation 2

What happened (the trigger)?

What did I think and how did I behave?

Which Prompt(s) activated?

Chapter 5. Impact of childhood Golden Rules
—

Part of understanding your Prompts and behavioural responses is to recognise the impact of any Golden Rules instilled by parents and other figures of authority during childhood. Such rules can be described in the acronym SMOGs: Shoulds, Musts, Oughts, Got-tos. They come with a conditional assumption, 'If... then...'. Whether spoken or unspoken, i.e. simply part of the 'norm' behaviour expected, they powerfully influence the way you think and respond to people and situations as an adult. Prompts can go off when a Rule is breached, either because you are unable to live up to it or others do not attain your standard of expectation. Once you recognise what has activated, you can choose to respond in a positive way.

I grew up with a strong Golden Rule: 'Treat others as you want to be treated.' If I am around someone who, in my opinion, breaches this rule I must be aware they may hold it with a different regard and not judge their response. How they handle a situation may be disrespectful in my eyes but I must not make the situation worse by reacting inappropriately. Equally, if I breach my own Rule that can cause me to react. Either way, it is important how I manage my 'Respect' Prompt so that I handle such situations positively. Similarly, I recognise other people do not have the same standard of punctuality drilled into them, the 'Better to be five minutes early than five minutes late!' Rule. I can choose to manage 'my stuff' and be gracious around others' lateness. Even when required to challenge someone regarding their lack of respect or poor punctuality it is about confronting the issue in a positive way so that the individual does not feel personally attacked.

Clients are often amused at the following list, wondering what it has to do with the way they communicate, influence and lead others. I love those moments when the light bulb turns on and they suddenly make a connection. So please bear with me!

Activity: Identifying your childhood Golden Rules

Look through the following list of Golden Rules and tick those that you can relate to. There is space to add any that you feel are not listed.

Golden Rule	Tick
Treat others as you would want to be treated	
Don't be selfish (put others first not just yourself)	
Always be polite and considerate	
Mind your manners: say please and thank you	
Be respectful (no answering back or rudeness)	
'I want' never gets (ask nicely)	
Speak when you are spoken to (do not interrupt)	
Children should be seen and not heard	
No showing off (people will think you are a big-head)	
Keep everything clean and tidy (keep up appearances)	
Never hang dirty washing in public (happy face)	
Always tell the truth	
If you make a promise, keep it	
Be loyal to those around you	
Act sensibly and take responsibility for your actions	
Finish what is on your plate	
Only leave the table when everyone has finished	
Finish what you have started (not half a job)	
If you do something, do it properly	
If you want something doing right, do it yourself	
Work hard and always do your best	
Work hard and you will get to where you want to be	
Work hard to earn your status/prove yourself	
There's no such thing as can't	
Failure is not an option (... it shows weakness)	
Have a go or you may regret it if you don't	

Golden Rule	Tick
If you're not happy about something, do something about it	
Time efficiency (make the most of every opportunity)	
Be on time and do not keep others waiting	
Be strong, do not show your weaknesses	
Stick up for yourself/do not let people walk over you	
Be careful who you trust (never trust anyone)	
Men/women/others have it easier	

Now you have identified your childhood Golden Rules the fun part is identifying how, as an adult, they affect your responses to others. Let me illustrate through a couple of client stories.

Client A identified with the Golden Rule, 'Finish what is on your plate' and when asked how it affected his approach to leadership, he suddenly looked rather sheepish and responded, 'I'm going to have to apologise to someone when we have finished.' Prior to our Monday morning meeting my client had had 'a bit of a go' at someone for not completing a task before leaving on Friday. The job did not need to be finished then, but in his eyes the plate had not been emptied. There was a learnt pattern of behaviour of expecting himself to do everything on his list and in the in-tray before going home, often resulting in him working long hours, which he was inappropriately imposing on others. The lesson was not only greater awareness of how he leads but the impact of the unrealistic expectations he puts on himself.

Client B fell quiet as she read the words, 'Children should be seen and not heard' and 'Speak when you are spoken to (do not interrupt)'. She suddenly remembered Sunday afternoons visiting her grandparents. Whilst her granny got the tea, she was expected to play in a separate room, only joining the adults when tea was served. Though her memories of her grandpa were of a kindly man, it was the custom to wait for him to speak and then politely respond. My client looked at me and exclaimed, 'That's what I do with those in authority, I wait for a director to invite me into the conversation instead of contributing when I have something valid to say'. This is what we call a 'set-up', i.e. when we are following a childhood Golden Rule today. In her case this manifested itself as holding back contributions at a senior level that colleagues not only wanted, but expected.

The following activity gives you the opportunity to explore the link between your Golden Rules and how they affect your ability to communicate, influence and lead others.

Activity: How my Golden Rules play out today

Record your most significant Golden Rules from the previous activity. Consider how these affect the way you communicate, influence and lead.

Golden Rule	How it impacts the way I communicate, influence and lead
1	
2	

Golden Rule	How it impacts the way I communicate, influence and lead
3	
4	
5	
6	
7	
8	
9	
10	

Chapter 6. Projection and reflection
—

Consider the following:

> "The more I believe it the more I see it,
> And the more I see it, the more I believe it."

In other words, as your beliefs about yourself begin to become entrenched, your perception of the world around is changed in a way that reinforces those beliefs:

I decide something looks this way

↓

So, I believe it is this way

↓

Then I see examples of it being this way

↓

THEN I GO OUT INTO THE WORLD AND UNCONCIOUSLY LOOK FOR EXAMPLES TO PROVE IT IS THIS WAY

↓

NOW I GET FURTHER CONFIRMATION I AM RIGHT

You do not look for evidence that does not support your belief system because you are already blinkered. You focus on all the things that confirm your beliefs and Prompts; your brain then tells you how right you are. As events occur, you dip in and out of your filed belief system to see where you have experienced this before and seek to prove it's right – repeatedly.

For example, if you have a Not Good Enough Prompt you look for evidence to prove you are not good enough. You see everything in the world that reinforces you are not good enough. You see the world through our own unique set of Not Good Enough spectacles! Such Prompts control your inner narrative, which in turn distorts your understanding and responses to events around you. Unconsciously, you flash your signals into society and the person or people who are most attracted to that signal will appear, usually those that have the same or completely opposite belief system. Though not your intention, such confused signals can result in dischord rather than than the empathy and harmony you were seeking.

Imagine if I introduced myself from my unique negative lens: 'Hello, I am stupid and not good enough, I can feel disregarded and have to be perfect, strong and responsible at all times, pleased to meet you!' You might think me crazy but this is what I could easily do, verbally or non-verbally, if I am not managing my emotional intelligence.

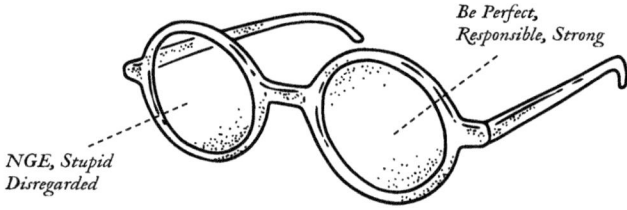

Be Perfect, Responsible, Strong

NGE, Stupid Disregarded

What you put into a relationship is what you get out. Similarly, in terms of projection, what you project into any situation or interaction is what gets reflected back to you. The question is, what are you projecting?

Activity: What I project

Write your 'introductions' based on your identified belief lens. (See how crazy it would be to live from this narrative!)

Chapter 7. Trace the triggers
—

Now you have begun to identify your Prompts, Golden Rules and what you are projecting through them, the next step is to begin to identify the daily effects of your emotional intelligence. The Trace the Triggers form enables you to piece together your repeat patterns of thinking in response to various external triggers, using actual scenarios. I encourage you to use the form regularly until you get to the point when you do not need it because you have committed it to memory. You may find it helpful to have a photo of it to work through when something happens rather than trying to remember later. There is no shortcut to understanding your emotional intelligence so be disciplined in using the form. Whether you prefer to think about or write examples, work through as many scenarios as possible recording any patterns that emerge – it will be worth it in the end!

In the next chapter, as you begin to understand how your emotional intelligence plays out, you will be able to shift your response to result in a more positive outcome but, for now, focus on what currently happens, however uncomfortable.

The following example illustrates what to record in each section. It is not intended to be prescriptive and the commentary would obviously differ from person to person. Your response to the same situation will look and feel different to that of others. Your starting point is to recognise when you are potentially tripping yourself up by allowing internal thoughts and emotions to dominate. Of course, the more copies of the form you complete the more you will begin to see patterns: which Prompts continuously cause a reaction and how you repeatedly respond. For example, is your response fight or flight? **Fight** response is when you display outwardly aggressive behaviour, attacking to defend your corner. Rather than outwardly attacking, you may fight back by adopting passive-aggressive behaviour, protesting through underhand methods such as voicing your opinion behind someone's back ('If it were me ...') or using other tactics such as slander, gossiping or moaning and groaning to others. **Flight** response causes you literally to retreat and shut down, not just from those involved in the situation but potentially others too.

Example Trace the Triggers form

What happened? (trigger)	*Colleagues have set up a project that is within my expertise without inviting me to be part of the team.*
What's the concern? (what I project)	*Why I have not been asked to join the project team. If I am not valued they may get rid of me at the next reorganisation.*
Thoughts about myself	*I feel unappreciated, I feel ignored, maybe I'm not as expert as I thought/good enough.*
Thoughts about others (that I keep to myself)	*How dare you ignore me. If it goes wrong do not blame me/come running to me.*
Emotions (however many)	*Unappreciated: sadness, fear.* *I feel ignored: sadness, anger, disgust.* *Not Good Enough: fear, shame, sadness.* *Job security: sadness, fear, panic.*
Prompts	*Unappreciated: Disregarded, Alone.* *Ignored: Disregarded, Respect, Loyalty.* *Not Good Enough: Stupid.* *Job security: Alone, Powerless.*

How did I react?	*I shut down and ignored everyone.*
Result (what I reflected back)	*Colleagues have not noticed how I feel, which makes me feel even more undervalued and questioning my ability.*

The signals you project both verbally and non-verbally influence what the world reflects back: it becomes a self-fulfilling prophecy! As you complete the Trace the Triggers form recognise your part (projection) and the impact it had (reflection).

Activity – Trace the Triggers form

What's happened? (The trigger)

What's the concern? (My Projection)

	What emotion do you feel? (Please tick the boxes)					
	Love / Joy	Sadness	Guilt / Shame	Anger / Disgust	Fear / Panic	
Thoughts about Myself						Prompt(s)
Thoughts about others						Prompt(s)

How did I react?

Result (my reflection on the outcome)

Trace the Triggers form observations

After completing a number of Trace the Triggers forms, record your observations below: a summary of the inner beliefs, thoughts and emotions that are regularly brought to the surface and your response patterns (e.g. fight-or-flight behaviour).

Summary

—

Let us reflect on what you have covered in Part 1:

- Emotional intelligence is distinct from intellect and personality. It is the faculty to interpret and express emotions.

- From the day you were conceived your memory files everything you experience: what happens to you, what is said, what you see, hear, smell and feel, both actual and perceived. All your memories and the subsequent thoughts about yourself and the world around you begin to create your own, unique, belief system.

- As your beliefs and thoughts accumulate, you begin to perceive patterns and make decisions about how you see yourself and how you believe the world will respond to you. Such beliefs and thoughts solidify, creating various response patterns.

- Thoughts (Prompts) and Golden Rules learnt in childhood, either spoken or the unspoken 'rules of the house', become your well-travelled pathways between the rational and emotional centres of your brain. These pathways affect the way you respond to people and situations every day.

- Emotional Intelligence is about managing your beliefs, thoughts and emotions that fill the gap between a trigger and how you ultimately respond.

- What you project into the world changes what is reflected back by others you encounter: 'The more I believe it, the more I see it and the more I see it, the more I believe it.' Such projection can be positive or negative and, either way, can have an adverse effect on relationships. By changing your internal thinking and what you project, you can change the 'outer aspects' of your life.

Part 2

Manage your emotional intelligence
—

Chapter 8. Redefine 'The Gap'

—

Understanding what is stored in your belief system and your well-worn pathways to reactions means you can now begin to change how you respond to any challenging trigger by redefining 'The Gap'.

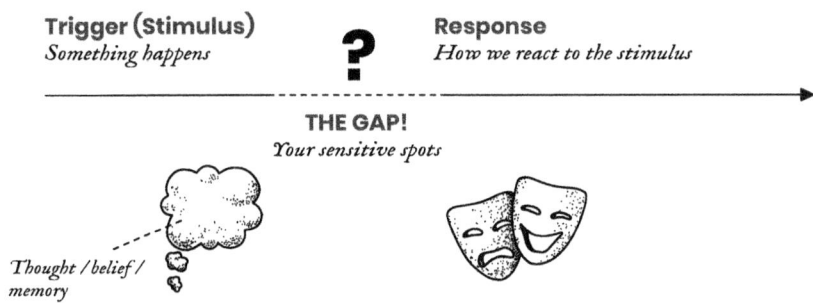

Revisiting the example Trace the Triggers form, how would the same scenario unfold if the individual had a greater awareness of their emotional intelligence? Let us replay the same scenario from the point of realising the concern but then choosing to manage any reactions by making a choice to 'manage my stuff'.

What happened? (trigger)	*Colleagues have set up a project that is my expertise area without inviting me to be part of the team.*
What's the concern? (what I project)	*Why I have not been asked to join the project team. If I am not valued they may get rid of me at the next reorganisation.*
Thoughts about myself	*Thoughts are surfacing around am I good enough and am I valued? However, I know I have expertise that can help.*

Thoughts about others (that I keep to myself)	*Whilst negative thoughts are circling, I am also considering other explanations so that I do not spiral into negativity. For example, they may intend to include me when the time is right. From previous conversations and experiences, I know they value my expertise.*
Emotions (however many)	*I recognise I am feeling sad, angry and fearful and if I'm not careful my fear will turn to panic around job security. I can manage these feelings until I resolve the situation.*
Prompts	*I recognise my Prompts i.e. Disregarded, Alone, Respect, Loyalty, Not Good Enough, Stupid, Powerless, but I can process 'my stuff' to enable me to resolve the situation.*
How did I react?	*I went and had a chat with the Project Lead who explained the full scope of the project. She apologised for not speaking to me earlier and was delighted to include me into the workstream that uses my expertise.*
Result (what I reflected back)	*Colleagues have valued my insight as an 'adviser' for the elements of the project where my expertise is needed and I have been able to support them and deliver other work. It has been a good experience.*

Your thoughts and emotions are what you project into a situation even before you open your mouth. It is important to process how you feel but at the same time, learn how to move forward in a way that builds relationships with others. Remember, you have been programmed to think and respond in certain ways. Actual or perceived negative experiences have created unhelpful beliefs that set your expectations.

The good news is that, **over time, you can begin to rewrite any negative belief to a more positive one,** which in turn changes your expectation, and therefore your experiences (from captivity to freedom).

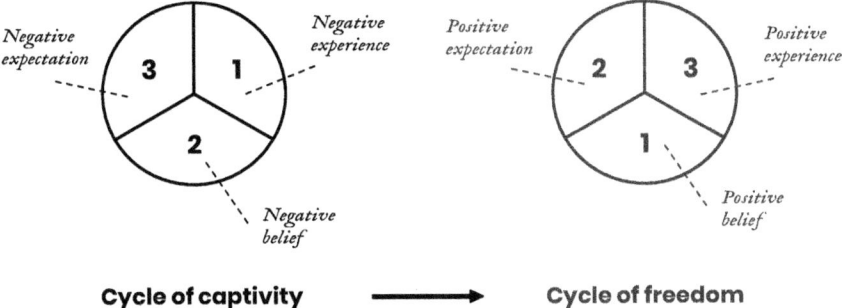

Cycle of captivity ⟶ **Cycle of freedom**

There will be two or three dominant thought patterns that get activated, often around fear of failure, unpredictability or rejection. Be aware of when you are reinforcing negative thoughts to yourself, thoughts that are simply lies you are believing, such as 'I'm so stupid' or 'No one cares'. Recognise you are living with the cycle of captivity and choose to shift your thinking and responses. For example, if you have a belief that 'Failure is not an option' it will hold you back from trying anything new in case you fail, but if you consciously rewrite that belief, to 'Failure is a chance to learn and grow' or 'Success is giving it a go,' you will shift your expectation and then your experience. Ask yourself, 'Is there a lie I am believing?' As your intuition reveals each lie, choose to reject and rewrite it with a positive truth. By shifting your beliefs, you will be better positioned to cultivate healthier relationships from a place of emotional maturity. Here are a few examples.

Old negative belief	New positive belief
Failure is not an option	Failure is a chance to learn and grow
Success is high attainment (top marks)	Success is giving it a go

I must work hard to get anywhere/ whatever I do must be perfect	I have done my best.
If you want something doing right, do it yourself	I can trust others to deliver good results
Finish everything on your plate	Prioritise and the rest can wait
Trust no one	I can build trust with those I choose to let into my life
Be strong, never show weakness	Openness draws people closer

Changing a belief to one that enables you to get more from life is rather like going to the gym: you do not see results instantly. Shifting a belief from negative to positive requires commitment to keep consciously correcting your thinking each time the old belief surfaces. By being intentional, you gradually begin to think differently and reap positive results because you are seeing yourself and the world around you in a new light.

Client C *had a crippling fear of failure, which meant he would not start anything he could not achieve. When it came to completing his professional qualification there was one unit he felt he could not attain and therefore he deployed avoidance tactics, even though not sitting the exam would mean having to do all the other units again! The 'Failure is not an option' belief was palpable and crippling. His first step was to recognise where he had learnt such a limiting belief; it was from well-intentioned parents and teachers who had labelled him a 'high achiever' leading to fear of disappointing those in authority and rejection if he did not achieve top marks. His second step was to acknowledge he was holding himself back out of fear, grappling with disappointment and frustration (anger) at himself. Such fear was projected through his 'flight' behaviour, much to the confusion of those who believed in him and wanted him to succeed. His third step was to make the decision to stop sabotaging himself and work towards a new belief: 'Success is giving it a go!' He booked the exam and each time the negative inner voice surfaced he shut it down with that new belief. Though there were times when old thinking surfaced, gradually his new belief took root and he began to feel comfortable that if he did not pass it was not the end of the world; he had given it a go and could always retake. To complete the story, he passed first time and his career has continued to flourish.*

This is a journey you can also take to remove any limiting beliefs and replace them with healthier ones that enable you to enjoy all life has to offer. **Affirmations** help purify your thoughts and restructure the dynamic of your brain so that you truly begin to think differently. The word affirmation comes from the Latin 'affirmare', originally meaning 'to make steady, strengthen'. Affirmations strengthen you by shifting your thinking from an old to a new belief.

Activity: Affirmations

Identify a new belief you wish to introduce.

Write the affirmation of that 12 times: 4 using your name, 4 using 'I', 4 using 'He/She'.

Example 1
Today Karen can experience success by giving new things a go x4
Today I can experience success by giving something new a go x4
Today she can experience success by giving something new a go x4

Example 2 (The 'XYZ' can vary but the principle is to focus on a realistic list and the rest can wait)
Today Karen can prioritise 'XYZ' and that will be enough x4
Today I can prioritise 'XYZ' and that will be enough x4
Today she can prioritise 'XYZ' and that will be enough x4

Ideally, aim to do this 4 times a week for 4–6 weeks. As you do so you will realise the negative internal voice is silenced and the new belief begins to take root!

Chapter 9. Your Belief Tree

—

Consider this: 'A good tree cannot bear bad fruit and a bad tree cannot bear good fruit. Every tree that does not bear good fruit is cut down and thrown into the fire.'[5]

Imagine yourself as a fruit tree. All that is above ground level reflects your outward behaviour seen by others. The roots of the tree are your inner beliefs, inner vows and deep-rooted judgements that feed your outward behaviour. To change the pattern of your outward behaviour towards people and situations, you must understand what lies at the root, cut it off and replace with truth. Then truth will flourish. Of course, some truths are not so positive, for example 'I'm not an amazing tennis player yet.' It is OK to accept this and get more tennis lessons, enjoy playing for the experience without needing to be number 1 and/or focus your energies elsewhere.

Inner beliefs are those thought patterns that are so real to you they impact on how you respond to people and situations (e.g. 'To achieve anything I'm going to have to work twice as hard as anyone else').

Inner vows are a defence mechanism you employ as a response to negative words, experiences, or situations to protect yourself from being hurt again (e.g. 'I'll never speak up again' (to avoid embarassment), 'I'll never trust you again' (to avoid being hurt), 'I'll always be grateful' (to avoid admonishment)).

Deep-rooted judgements are critical, condemning judgements of others and a refusal or an inability to forgive or rethink (e.g. 'Men cannot be trusted').

Drawing your own Belief Tree brings together many of the concepts explored in earlier chapters and enables you to visualise how they link together to form your emotional intelligence. This is rather like putting together the pieces of a jigsaw and discovering the overall picture. Just remember, each time you peel a layer of your emotional intelligence onion, your Belief Tree may need to be updated. Like an actual tree, your Belief Tree is constantly developing as you become more self-aware. Here is an example tree to illustrate how your thoughts, emotions, Golden Rules and beliefs connect, determining your outward behaviour.

Example Belief Tree Illustration

Outward behaviour (what others see/sense)

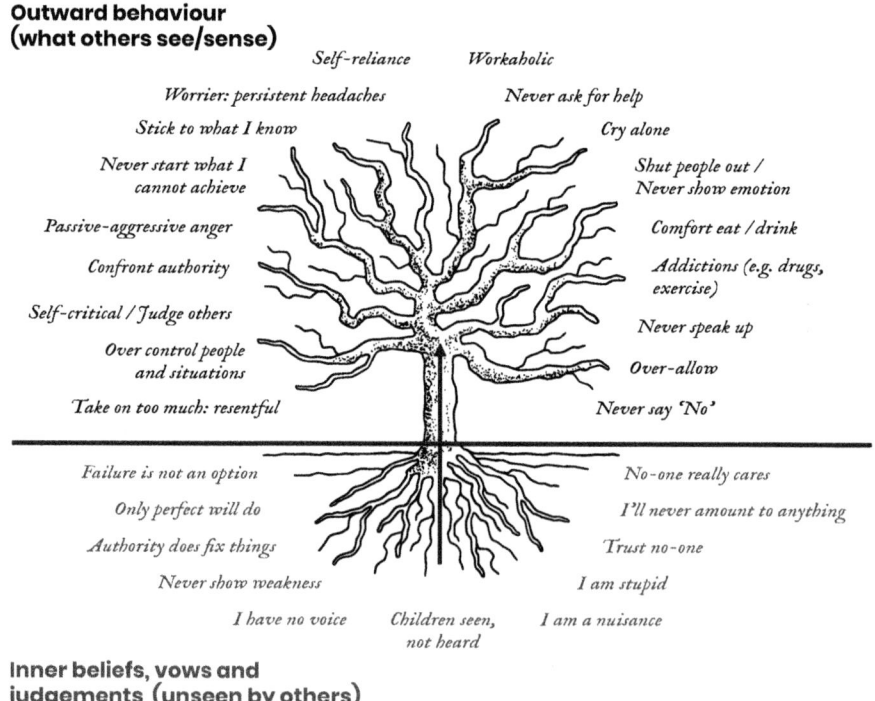

Self-reliance Workaholic

Worrier: persistent headaches Never ask for help

Stick to what I know Cry alone

Never start what I cannot achieve Shut people out / Never show emotion

Passive-aggressive anger Comfort eat / drink

Confront authority Addictions (e.g. drugs, exercise)

Self-critical / Judge others Never speak up

Over control people and situations Over-allow

Take on too much: resentful Never say 'No'

Failure is not an option No-one really cares

Only perfect will do I'll never amount to anything

Authority does fix things Trust no-one

Never show weakness I am stupid

I have no voice Children seen, not heard I am a nuisance

Inner beliefs, vows and judgements (unseen by others)

Activity: My Belief Tree

Begin to create your own Tree, considering your Prompts, Golden Rules and behaviours alongside the inner beliefs, vows and judgements that are at the root. One belief can have an impact on four different outward behaviours. Similarly, three beliefs can link to one behaviour. What is important is to identify the correlation between the inner processing and outward behaviours. As you continue to mature your emotional intelligence keep updating your tree. Gradually, it will shift from negative to positive and good fruit will flourish.

**Outward behaviour
(what others see/sense)**

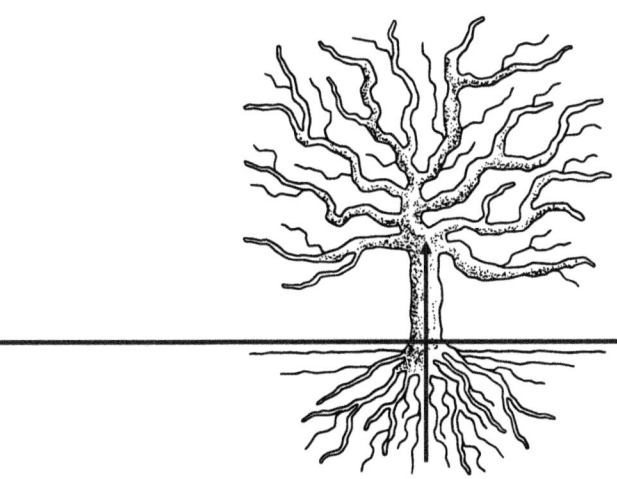

**Inner beliefs, vows and
judgements (unseen by others)**

Chapter 10. How to connect with your emotions
—

Connecting

Emotions aren't right or wrong; only actions can be judged. What is important to understand is why you sometimes struggle to connect with your feelings. Here are some examples.

You have learnt to live by someone else's feelings.

Client D recalled how she would gauge her father's mood when he arrived home from work. If he appeared tired and grumpy, she returned to her bedroom to ensure he could not 'pick a fight' over something that she had or had not done that day. If he appeared jovial, she would rush downstairs to greet him. This affected her performance as a manager because she responded to others from a learnt behaviour associated with authority, to steer clear if the 'mood music' around someone felt unsafe. It meant she struggled to challenge issues that needed addressing because of the fear there would be negative repercussions.

Your family discouraged the expression of feelings.

Many people learn to rationalise a situation (often illogically, rather than logically) when they are emotionally charged, rather than allow themselves to process how they truly feel. An example is when someone elderly dies. Often the rational brain concludes they had a good life and it is their time to depart this world but such a response allows no space to grieve.

You were taught emotions are good or bad.

Love and Joy are 'good' and anger, disgust, sadness, guilt, shame, fear and panic are 'bad' that are either stifled or ignored because we do not know what to do with them. This is unhelpful because emotions simply help us to be aware of what we feel. Telling children anger is bad shuts them down and they grow to be an adult who does not know how to handle anger. Have you ever been in a supermarket and witnessed an exhausted mum at the end of her tether telling her ranting, tear-stained toddler how naughty they are and to behave? Remember, in that moment the child will pick up mum's disgust and anger rather than her tiredness, embarrassment and exasperation at their behaviour. Maybe you have been there yourself! Before I had children, my thought would have been 'Can't you control your child?' because I was taught anger is bad. However, the more I have learnt about emotional intelligence and my own experiences of having a strong-willed child, the more I have realised anger isn't good or bad. It is important to teach a child how to express any emotion safely through listening to their needs, as is being aware of the messages (verbal and non-verbal) communicated to a child.

You may have experienced chronic shock and your emotions are 'stuck'

Like a speedometer after a car crash, any form of emotional, physical or sexual abuse, neglect or major trauma may have fractured your ability to process at an emotional level. In these circumstances, it is important to seek professional help and support from a qualified therapist or psychologist – a big ask when trust may have been broken.

Coping strategies

Throughout your childhood you will have been exposed to various influencers who have taught you how to disconnect from or ignore your emotions. Which of the following strategies have you learnt that enable you to stay out of touch with your emotions?

Intellectualisers keep conversations on rational things. When emotions surface, you talk until you cannot feel them anymore.

Intellectualisers stick to talking about surface issues, such as the weather, current affairs, facts over feelings, for example 'He was eighty-five, so his death was to be expected. Weren't we lucky with the weather today?'

Minimising downplays any emotions and you will use excuses such as 'Yes, my Dad often told me I wouldn't amount to much, but he was right on most things,' to avoid having to process how you truly feel.

Denial is another method, literally denying emotions even exist. Instead, you rationalise your responses rather than allow yourself to feel your own feelings. For example, disappointment you were overlooked for a promotion will be explained using such words as 'I didn't think I would get the job anyway.'

Swallowing is a physical response to dissipate any emotion that is trying to surface. Tears or feeling angry are suppressed by taking a deep breath, swallowing, or sighing deeply.

Isolating is a method used to create and/or retreat to your own private, imaginary world. You escape into fiction and mentally you are miles away.

Taking care of others takes the focus off you and firmly places it onto how others are feeling. By doing this you do not have to process how you feel. Useful phrases, such as 'Enough about me, what about you?' guide any interaction to a one-sided conversation, thus keeping your feelings buried.

Activity: How I disconnect with my emotions

Which methods do I use to stay out of touch with my emotions? (It may also be helpful to refer to the activity in Chapter 4 – How I react to my Prompts)

Chapter 11. How to manage your emotions

—

Emotions are not poisonous plants to be eradicated. They are like wild plants ready to be cultivated. It is important to cultivate our responses to all our emotions, particularly anger, because when left unchecked it can have such a detrimental, lasting impact. Learning to cultivate your response to anger will help you to maintain a healthier relationship with yourself (because we often turn our anger against ourselves) and those around us.

Understanding and managing anger

We all experience the emotion of anger but how we display it will vary from person to person. Your upbringing will affect how you express anger, mainly learning from key influencers what they believe is acceptable and what is not. Many of us are taught anger is bad so we try to dumb it down or ignore it, in the hope it will go away. Unfortunately, such a strategy does not work! Anger pops up when you least expect it, often disproportionately to the 'crime' committed. Of course, what people consider to be inappropriate anger may also differ!

Client E *was 'sent' for remedial coaching because of his aggressive behaviour and 'rudeness' to members of his team, which had resulted in a grievance against him and a subsequent written warning. After a ten-minute, angry rant during which I listened carefully to any verbal clues he gave about his emotional intelligence, I responded by compassionately saying, 'I'm so sorry you feel misunderstood and not listened to. What can I do to support you?' His demeanour immediately shifted, rather like the wind dropping from the sails of a boat and we began the journey of exploring his emotional intelligence, unpacking why he felt this way. What surfaced was that he came from an extremely large family and had learnt that 'If you don't shout loudly, you will not be heard'. What others defined as anger was simply him positioning himself to be heard! Other basic etiquettes of politeness had also not been taught in his childhood, for example holding open a door for others and good time-keeping, which was why he was perceived by others to be not only aggressive but also rude. Awareness around his emotional intelligence and adjusting certain behaviours enabled him to improve work relationships.*

I have a heart-felt belief that people do not arrive at work with the intention to get angry and behave aggressively towards others. Something happens and they enter The Gap, responding out of 'their stuff' with anger (frustration, irritation, annoyance). All human beings experience the emotion of anger, it is part of who we are, but how we deal with it will vary.

Exploders (or outwardly aggressive) are passive until they become activated and they blow up with a huge outburst, which is usually out of proportion to the 'crime'. In its extreme form exploders kill others but most rant and rage or slam doors. Exploders immediately feel much better after such an outburst, with a sense of relief they have expressed how they feel to everyone around. The problem is the collateral damage done to the people around them. Over time the receivers of such a tirade start to resent or fear the exploder and they will distance themselves from contact with that individual whenever possible.

Underminers (or passively aggressive) are passive and seemingly agreeable on the outside, but aggressive on the inside. They use sneaky attacks to wound and 'get even' due to fear of genuine confrontation. They also use an array of tactics in order to satisy their anger: humour, gossip, slander behind a person's back, quiet rebellion and 'go slow work ethic', and ignoring people, requests, or instructions.

Client F contacted me out of desperation following a relationship breakdown between two senior consultants who led a key department at a hospital. Things had deteriorated to the point where they avoided one another, which was making the department dysfunctional. The longer-serving clinician had adopted passive-aggressive tactics to try and take back full control by turning others against his colleague. He was undermining his authority as co-lead and generally making inappropriate comments and accusations. In contrast, the other clinician had adopted 'flight' behaviour, shutting down and minimising conversation with anyone else. In working with each clinician to explore their emotional intelligence, issues around control and authority came up for both. The longer-serving and older of the two was raised in a family where respect to elders was all important. He had recruited the other clinician to bring fresh ideas into the department but when he started to do this, he reacted because he felt he was losing control. He acknowledged his belief around 'authority has the last word'. In contrast, the younger clinician resented 'Being told what to do,' a reminder of his own father who had been controlling and often made him feel inadequate, ignored and unloved. Two senior clinicians operating out of childhood memories and beliefs that were negatively affecting the progress of an entire department! As both began to 'own their part' they were able to reconcile their differences and apologise to the senior nursing team and junior doctors for not leading in the best way. Whilst they were unlikely to head to the pub for a drink together, they developed an understanding of how they could best work together to improve the performance of the department, much to the relief of the Chief Executive (who had intervened) and their staff.

Self-punishers are those who always feel everything is their fault. They are frequently depressed, with a sense of self-loathing and hating themselves. They turn other people's inappropriate behaviour on themselves, for example when a partner or boss gets angry, it must be my fault for whatever reason. Their self-confidence and self-esteem are low and often manifest through Unworthy, Unloved, Unlovable, Not Good Enough Prompts.

Somatisers use their body to defuse anger or attempt to take back control, for example overeating, smoking, drinking, taking drugs, over-exercising to a point when they cannot stop. They may also turn to self-harm or attempt suicide.

Client G immediately recognised a pattern between feeling Not Good Enough, Inadequate, Unworthy and Unsupported and comfort eating to make herself feel better. When activated, usually when people had been critical, she ate to comfort and reward herself in the hope she would feel better but ended up feeling worse because she put on weight. She had spent years on fad diets unaware of the link between food and her emotional intelligence. The learnt behaviour to 'reward when feeling low' to suppress her feelings of anger began as a child, buying sweets to buffer the effects of her mother's harsh words, which created the belief that 'Whatever I do will never be enough!' This left her feeling miserable and isolated. Using the Trace the Triggers form, a new belief that 'I am worth it' and a list of positive activities for when she felt overwhelmed (meeting a friend, a relaxing bath, doing something creative) enabled her to sustain healthier eating habits, manage her weight and feel more confident. She openly admitted she had become easier to work with as a result because she had a more positive disposition and felt better in herself. In her own words: 'Nobody wants to work with a grouch!'

Anger, hostility and hate

Before moving on, let me take a minute to differentiate between anger, hostility and hate to avoid any confusion.

Anger is an emotion and it is neutral. You can love someone and still be angry with them. Anger is a powerful emotion that tells you something is wrong, that you need to act in some way. Anger gets a bad reputation because, whilst it can be expressed constructively, it is often displayed in an inappropriate, sadly destructive way.

Hostility is an attitude. Hostile people have developed a negative attitude to persons or events and such an attitude is never constructive but simply destroys. When hostility is left to harden over time it turns into **hate**. Hostility and hate cause many of the societal issues at both a micro and macro level.

Activity: How I manage my anger

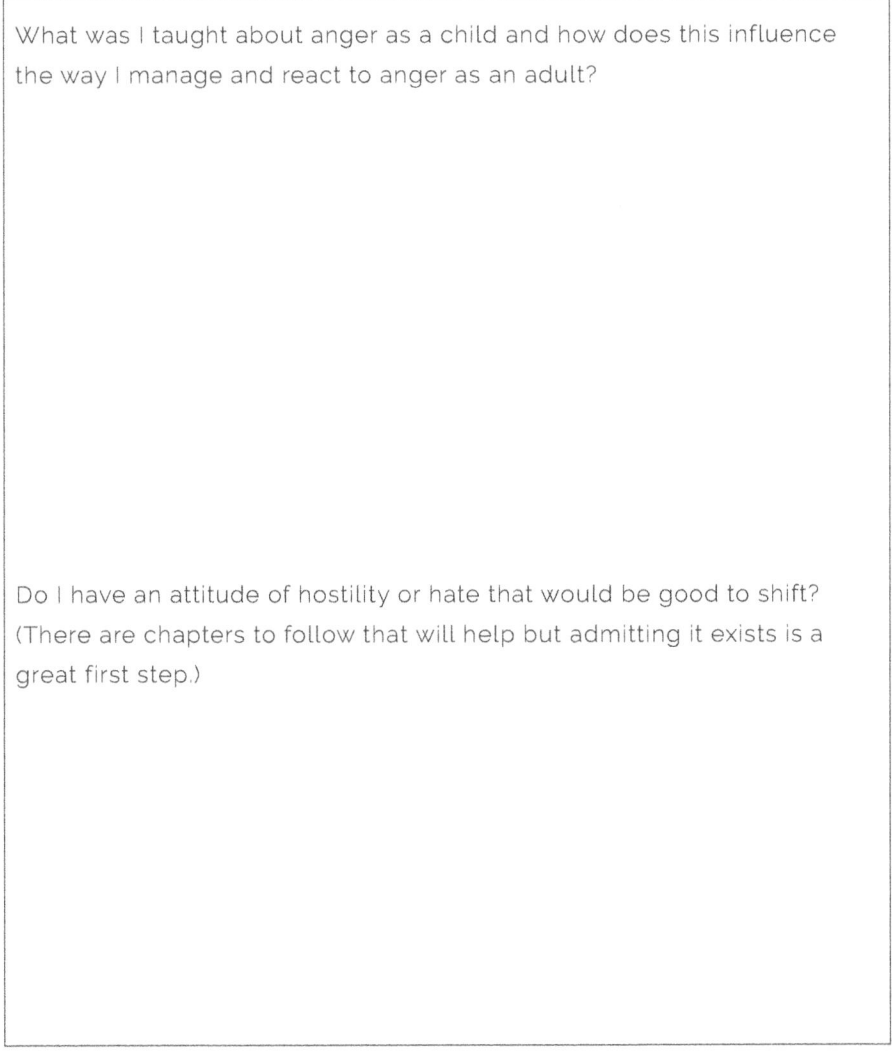

What was I taught about anger as a child and how does this influence the way I manage and react to anger as an adult?

Do I have an attitude of hostility or hate that would be good to shift? (There are chapters to follow that will help but admitting it exists is a great first step.)

Emotional Management

Here are three steps you can take to help manage the array of emotions you might experience in a healthier way.

1.   **Recognise** your feelings by admitting them to yourself, for example 'I feel angry' rather than trying to ignore, disguise or rationalise them. Maybe someone has criticised you unfairly or gossiped about you. Allow yourself time to feel your feelings, for example how hurt and upset you feel, your anger, fear, sadness and disappointment.

2.   **Exercise self-control.** This is not about shutting your emotions down and pretending they are not there but learning how to push the pause button on the situation until such time as you can process how you are feeling. If you respond in the moment when you are emotionally out of control you risk making the situation worse and breaking trust with others who are directly or indirectly involved. Remember the Trace the Triggers form on page 50, use it as you pause to recognise what is happening in your internal narrative.

Client H had no pause mechanism but would fly off the handle when he felt his boss, peers or family were 'ganging up against him'. He grew up as one of four brothers in a home that lacked a good fatherly role model. The four boys would 'fight it out' to gain supremacy. Whilst he had many good leadership qualities, when my client felt outnumbered and under threat the 'fight your corner' Golden Rule would manifest because of the belief that 'No one's got my back'. By understanding his Not Good Enough, Stupid, Unlovable and Out of Control Prompts he was able to recognise when they were igniting and choose to manage his responses in the moment, so that he did not lash out against those who disagreed with him. How he was feeling was simply a warning light to 'his stuff' that he could safely process later. Over time his previous volatile responses significantly diminished to the point when colleagues would listen to his suggestions because he presented his ideas positively rather than aggressively, which had previously pushed people away in fear and disgust at his behaviour. On the odd occasion that a little kick back occurred, everyone was able to joke about it in a way that maintained dignity and respect because he had taken ownership of his behaviour.

3. **Express** emotion in a safe way that does not push people away and/or hurt them. You can use an array of techniques alongside the Trace the Triggers form to help you process and let go of negative thoughts and emotions.

   Dancing, drumming and boxing (using imaginary drum or punch bag in front of you). This helps to circulate the neuropeptides around the body and shift any emotion you are experiencing. If any of your Prompts are activated at work, lock yourself in a toilet cubicle and try this – it works!

   Client J maintained professional composure at work but was concerned how he subsequently took out all his frustration on his young family on arriving home. A simple request was met with a grumpy, aggressive response making his young sons apprehensive around him, which was upsetting. I suggested a boxing bag, which he purchased and hung in the garage. As he arrived home, he entered the house via the garage, putting on his boxing gloves to dispose of any anger that had accumulated during the day. Not only did his relationship with his wife and sons improve, but he also noticed the benefits in the way he handled pressure and responded to colleagues at work because he was safely discharging his emotions on a regular basis.

   Other physical exercise has a similar impact and benefits, to both your physical and mental well-being.

Ranting! Think about a child having a huge meltdown. Part of you thinks 'how inappropriate' but there is a part of you that thinks 'I wish I could do that!' You can, simply by lying in the middle of your bed and safely thrash out how you are feeling. Alternatively, scream everything you need to say into a pillow until there is nothing left and you are at the end of your 'feel'. I know this sounds a little weird, but far better to shout at a pillow than a loved one or a work colleague! This is also a great method to teach children how to safely discharge their anger. Having let go of their anger they will find it easier to calm down and talk about their thoughts and feelings.

Take 10 deep breaths, exhaling all the anger, disappointment, resentment, etc. and inhaling truth in how you choose to see yourself and the situation.

Laughter is a wonderful tonic against any negative thoughts your internal voice is transmitting. As you recognise a negative thought pattern, laugh at it because it is a lie. Immediately replace it with a truth, for example 'I am good enough, I can do this!' Laughter is also a great tonic to deal with any heaviness your internal narrative creates that literally weighs you down. Prompts that lead to that may be Duty, Responsible, Loyalty, Failure. When life has become too burdened and serious, inject some laughter and joy through watching videos, listening to music, etc. Sometimes we just need to lighten up and not take life so seriously.

*The first time I met **Client K** she literally walked into the room stooped over, like she was carrying the weight of the world on her shoulders. We identified Prompts relating to responsibility, duty and loyalty and a pattern of taking responsibility when it was not hers to carry. She acknowledged that life had been tough over several years, which had been made worse by trying to play the* *roles of superwoman and saviour both at work and in her personal life. As the eldest child having to 'Be sensible and set the example' and school reports that she 'Always works hard and can be relied on', helped create the beliefs that affected her behaviour, daily. I suggested she find something to put on her desk or carry around in her bag that would be a reminder to 'Lighten up and grow down' (i.e. to not take life so seriously). On the way home she saw a bright pink, feathered ostrich pen that bounced up and down when touched that instantly made her smile. Such a physical reminder on the desk helped her change her responses to people and situations and reminded her not to automatically take responsibility. I also gave her one of my favourite 'homework' ideas to combat taking life too seriously, encouraging her to skip like a little girl. Initially around the house then a few on the way to work, gradually increasing. I love it when clients take on such sillines because, when they do, it is liberating! Physiologically the 'lighter approach to life' saw her stand tall and discover laughter and joy once again. In her words: 'Life feels a lot better!'*

Sadness and tears are allowed because they help you express how you feel. Big boys and girls can cry, just be sensitive to the time and place and how much to express. There is a balance to ensuring your feelings are understood and ensuring others present do not become overwhelmed by them. If you are home and feeling sad, a good way to exercise this emotion is to watch something or listen to music that allows tears to flow alongside a good supply of tissues. Once you feel better and have processed what was happening (remember the Trace the Triggers form), then watch, listen to or do something more uplifting.

Spiritual prayer and/or meditation help to process and let go of negative thoughts and emotions. Always allow yourself to 'feel your feel' as you process your feelings, rather than use these methods simply to calm yourself down or 'empty yourself out'. Having finished processing, refill with positive truths!

I encourage you to adopt these techniques to help you to manage your emotions daily. Remember, emotions are not poisonous plants to be eradicated. They are like wild plants ready to be cultivated. Not processing and releasing your emotions will leave a residue, which accumulates over time, often affecting your body physiologically. Learning to cultivate your response to anger will help you to maintain a healthier relationship with yourself (because we often turn our anger against ourselves), and those around us. Processing your emotions safely will enable you to live a longer, healthier and most definitely happier life.

Activity: Managing my emotions differently

Which techniques do I use and which might be helpful to introduce to ensure I manage all my emotions safely?

Chapter 12. Building trust and the power of forgiveness
—

To develop a healthier, ongoing relationship with someone you need to build reciprocal trust. The ability to trust is rather like a muscle. For some it grows and strengthens early in childhood with only minor knocks and bruises from which they recover. For others, it gets damaged and does not develop properly, creating an inner belief that it is unsafe to trust anyone. As an adult it is important to make the choice to forgive those who have wronged you in the past and develop a habit of forgiving, even in the small things that occur every day, so that you can develop and maintain your ability to trust others.

There are a lot of misunderstandings about forgiveness that prevent people making a conscious decision to forgive. **Forgiveness is <u>not</u> saying, 'What you did is OK'**, it is about what you gain, rather than what you give up. The choice to forgive is simply declaring you are no longer going to be held hostage to the anger, disgust, fear, anxiety and panic that stem from what happened, both in the past or more recently. Forgiveness is about resigning your role as self-appointed judge and jury and leaving the courtroom! You may ask, 'Why should I let them off the hook?', (e.g. the teacher who ridiculed you, the bully, the boss who used you for personal gain, a controlling partner). But consider this: who is affected by what happened, you or the perpetrator? Ask yourself 'Who is on the hook?'

Forgiveness takes the sting out of the memory, enabling you to walk free and move forward. In contrast, unforgiveness allows someone to live rent-free in your head. It leaves you imprisoned, stuck 'on the hook', unable to enjoy and participate fully in life. Not forgiving can be associated with persistent mistrust, which can get in the way of building healthier relationships with others or letting go of control.

Client L struggled to build trust in any relationship, both at work and in his personal life, because of being badly bullied as a child and the school not handling the situation appropriately. Years later the trauma still had a daily effect, whilst the perpetrators lived free unaware of the consequences of their actions. By continuing to hold on to a limiting belief, 'Trust no one', the only person directly affected was my client and indirectly, his partner, friends, and work colleagues. Everyone was kept at a distance, resulting in a lack of relational connection with anyone and a feeling of isolation and loneliness, because 'No one cares'. It was important to make the decision to forgive, to release him from his self-imposed prison and slowly build greater trust and authenticity into all his relationships. Though not instant, the decision to forgive has made a difference and my client is living in a new, rather refreshing reality where people do care and want to support him, which has been life changing.

There are occasions when the person who has hurt you has not apologised or shown any remorse and it still feels unsafe to be around them. In such situations it may be necessary to create clear protective boundaries should you need to have contact with them. Just because you forgive someone does not mean you need to be in a relationship with them. Having forgiven, it may also be timely to end the connection.

To help you experience freedom from hurts from the past that have held you back and kept you prisoner and when it feels right for you to do so, work through the following steps. You may find it helpful to do this with the help of a good friend, relative, psychologist or specialist therapist.

Activity: How to forgive

1.   Record on a piece of paper the name of the person who hurt you.

2.   Write down everything that happened in the form of a letter to the person expressing how it made you feel. Don't worry, I am not going to ask you to send it! This exercise is purely for your benefit,

your chance to express your emotions and hurts, in the form of: 'Dear X, when you did/said this, it made me feel … .' For many this narrative is uncomfortable because it expresses what has been buried, often for years. Do not 'soften' your language, be brutally honest. Write down exactly how the experience has made you feel and its impact, both past and present, together with any fears for the future. (The technique of screaming in a pillow can help release any anger, fear, guilt and shame that comes up and have a supply of tissues for moments of sadness should the tears flow). Keep going until you have recorded everything that needs to be expressed.

3. Leave some time to further reflect – often the biggest revelation comes later! It can be helpful to conclude the letter with a final statement such as: 'The biggest point I want to make to you is …', folowed by, for example, 'You are a bully' or 'Your behaviour is not going to hold me back any longer' .

4. Once you feel you have covered everything and come to the end of your hurt, read your letter aloud (to yourself or maybe to a trusted friend, family member, therapist, or psychologist). Then write down and read aloud, 'X, I choose to forgive you.' Say this several times until it begins to feel real and there is a sense of freedom within you.

5. Take the letter and destroy it.

Chapter 13. Tackling busyness (prioritising)
—

There are many external factors that influence your pace of life. Your emotional Intelligence will be triggered constantly simply by the choices you make in how you spend your time. Equally, it can dictate how you spend time and the pace of life you set yourself because of your inner beliefs, thoughts and emotions. You can easily end up in a vicious cycle of reaction between the two: the external pressures of life and the internal battle of the mind.

*Over the years, **Client M** had worked his way up the corporate ladder and due to his professional experience and knowledge became known as 'The man to go to.' Such a 'saviour' accolade made him feel secure because he had made himself 'indispensable'. However, as colleagues left to go home only then did he begin his 'day job'. As the volume and intensity of work increased he began to work later and later into the evenings, trying to keep on top of everything to ensure he remained indispensable. Work then spilled into the weekend affecting his family. Operating in this way was unsustainable and he was at breaking point. It was important to differentiate the external pressure from the internal narrative: 'his stuff' around feeling 'not good enough' and 'unworthy' and 'I'll have to work hard to prove myself'. Pushing the pause button enabled him to recognise (and laugh at) the work–life pattern he had created and how his emotional intelligence was working to his and others' detriment. His actions were tipping him to overload but also stopping colleagues from developing and taking responsibility for their work. Coaching, supporting and delegating in a timely way empowered colleagues and won back precious time to complete his tasks within office hours. A win–win for everyone!*

The common denominator of the internal dialogue and external factors is an awareness of how you choose to value and prioritise time. It is very tempting to subscribe to busyness but when you do, relationships suffer, particularly when you focus on tasks and the many distractions of twenty-first century living over people.

Approval Strategies

How you choose to prioritise time links with various approval strategies learnt in childhood that contribute to your emotional intelligence. You may relate to one or more of these approval strategies and it is important to acknowledge how they influence you.

People Pleasers struggle to say 'No' because they do not want to disappoint others or appear, for example, inadequate or disloyal; however, they end up taking on too much, becoming stressed, irritable and/or shut down as they try to achieve everything they have unrealistically agreed to. Such a desire to please can manifest in any relationship but when work-driven it can have a detrimental impact on personal relationships.

Saviours love to play the hero, to be the solution and 'save the day', but the downside is that they take on too much, over-allow around others and easily end up feeling exhausted and resentful of people and the situation they have put themselves in.

Strivers have everything to prove and will over-allow to justify their worth. Their achievements will be numerous but often come at a cost in terms of relationships and health because time is prioritised to the tasks rather than the people and their well-being.

Procrastinators waste time making excuses to avoid making decisions because of several underlying reasons. Procrastination may arise from a fear of unpredictability and being overwhelmed by the enormity of getting to the end goal, believing it to be unachievable. There may also be fear of making a mistake and/or fear of failure and any subsequent rejection. The partnership of procrastination and perfectionism, when the individual is unwilling to start unless it can be done perfectly, can be crippling. Regardless of the underlying reasons for procrastination, it can be hard to step back from the emotional experience, process it and then move forward constructively, one step at a time.

Perfectionists waste precious time trying to make everything perfect rather than excellent. They believe that perfection is the key to success, acceptance, even survival. The alternative is mediocrity and failure. However, the alternative to the unrelenting pursuit of perfection is not no standards, it is high-but-achievable standards – not mediocrity but striving for excellence. As many authors have noted, striving for excellence is not the same as striving for perfection, the former is healthy and self-satisfying the latter unnattainable and people-pleasing.

You may find it interesting to explore further personality type indicators by completing an Enneagram personality test[6]. This aims to reveal how emotions drive your life and how you engage with others to get what you want and need. The Enneagram defines nine personality types, each with its own set of strengths, weaknesses and opportunities for personal development: The Perfectionist, The Giver, The Achiever, The Individualist, The Investigator, The Sceptic, The Enthusiast, The Challenger, The Peacemaker. Such a profile can help you 'position' where you are in terms of different personality types and how they potentially link to your emotional intelligence.

The Wheel of Reaction

Whatever your personality type and the approval strategies you adopt, be aware how they are expressed through any negative inner narrative you are believing from your Belief Tree. Like a hamster on a wheel, it is easy to become trapped in a vicious cycle known as the Wheel of Reaction because once you jump on, it can be difficult to get off! You sacrifice (over-allow) with the expectation others will be pleased that you have 'volunteered'. When your effort is not acknowledged (a thank you, a well done, appreciation from a family member, a pay rise, bonus, promotion, etc.) disappointment kicks in, your internal narrative activates Prompts and you react. Resentment and anger alongside an array of thoughts and other emotions take over. Your reactions put you on a collision course with yourself and others as you adopt fight or flight responses, until you begin to feel guilty about your behaviour. The emotion of guilt simply sets you up to sacrifice again and around the wheel you go.

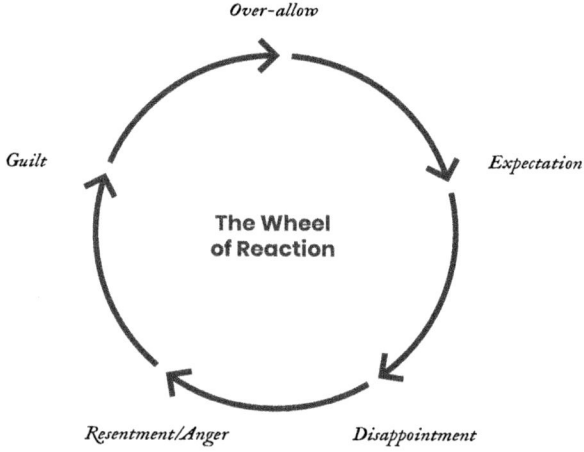

Over-allow

Guilt

The Wheel of Reaction

Expectation

Resentment/Anger

Disappointment

Client N identified his Wheel of Reaction since childhood. His father had grand plans for his only child but his behaviour towards him was based on control, with little encouragement or affection. Wanting to hear his father's approval meant he developed 'People Pleaser' and 'Striver' approval strategies in the hope his father would acknowledge an achievement. With every school exam and sports activity, he constantly over-allowed in the hope his performance would be applauded. Sadly, his endeavours met with criticism and an attitude of 'If you want to be the best you must try harder'. As an adult my client was his own worst critic. Whilst work was delivered to a high standard, he felt it was never quite good enough and any small suggestion for improvement led to disappointment and a self-fulfilling prophecy, 'To be the best I must try harder.' The cycle of trying harder but still feeling inadequate simply fuelled my client's anger and resentment against himself and those 'criticising' him. This in turn made him implode *and isolate himself from colleagues and family, leading to longer hours at work, which all finally caught up with him. He identified a new belief: 'What I have done is enough'. He gradually shifted his thinking and learnt to keep off the Wheel of Reaction by communicating his wants, needs and expectations to others more authentically. He continues to have a strong work ethic but has found greater balance between his career and personal life, concluding that **'Success does not necessarily bring fulfilment'**. The analogy that you can climb the ladder of success only to find it is up against the wrong wall resonated with him!*

As you develop your emotional intelligence, recognise when you are about to jump onto the Wheel of Reaction and rather than overcompensating by taking on too much, start by defining and communicating your expectations. Being genuine with others helps you to keep balanced and you are less likely to subscribe to self-inflicted busyness.

Busyness

Busyness can easily become a habit and an accolade, not just in the context of how we approach work but life in general. Think about it: when someone asks you how you are doing, is your answer 'OK, but very busy'? Your response to this may flow from your perception that there does not appear to be enough time in the day to do everything you need to do. You go to bed feeling you have not achieved enough, sometimes tossing and turning as you worry about the length of your to-do list. You wake up tired and fearing the onslaught of another day as you try once again to achieve everything you feel pressured to deliver. Without realising it, you are setting yourself up to fail. Stress and tension run high as you try to deliver the impossible, which impacts on relationships both at work and at home. It is time to acknowledge the fact that each day will always only ever have twenty-four hours, many of which are required to sleep and rest!

Busyness is more about what you focus on, and how you prioritise time rather than the result of the volume of work you attempt each day. You can be productive without falling into the trap of busyness; they are different. Instead of focusing and prioritising on what is most important, we easily get distracted, filling our day with tasks and activities that do not meet our goals and add little or no value. Such busyness is exacerbated by your internal narrative and an inability to say 'No', resulting in trying to achieve the impossible, which impacts on your emotional well-being. Prompts begin to be activated as you become more and more out of balance. The saying 'If you want something doing ask a busy person to do it' can be a millstone around your neck rather than an accolade! It can be helpful to use the Trace the Triggers form to identify any patterns you have created around busyness. Once you understand 'my stuff' that leads you to take on too much, you will be able to make the choice to respond differently and gradually rebalance your priorities.

Rocks, pebbles, sand

What you prioritise will look and feel different dependent on each stage of life. My life twenty years ago, balancing being a wife and mother of three young children with running a business, was different to life now and required a different approach to the way I planned and prioritised each day. Consider the following as a helpful metaphor for life. Imagine you have a jam jar containing rocks, pebbles, and sand. The rocks are the main priorities in your life, the pebbles are the other important things, and the sand grains are the minor things and potential distractions. If you put the sand in first, then the pebbles, you risk not being able to fit in the rocks. Place the rocks in first, then the pebbles with the sand added last to ensure the key priorities get the attention they require first. The sand can fit around the rocks and pebbles or be left out altogether. You may also discover certain pebbles can wait until tomorrow!

Learn self-discipline with how and when you work, rest and play, continuously reviewing the contents of your 'jar of life' and not trying to put too much in. How can you be productive but balanced, both physically and emotionally? This will be different for you compared to others and at different stages of your life, but it is important to find your own equilibrium.

External drivers

24/7 technology access means you can be contacted by anyone at any hour of the day or night, particularly when no boundaries have been agreed. Constant access to laptops and mobile phones makes it harder to switch off. People assume you are available, which you prove to be correct by responding. Simple steps can ensure you maintain greater daily balance.

1. **Turn off all notifications** including emails, both on your laptop and mobile phone so you have control over what you look at and when, rather than constant interruptions. Whether you are focusing on a particular work task or prioritising an evening with family and friends, be more disciplined around when you respond to avoid sabotaging your plans.

2. **Out-of-hours messaging** for your laptop and phone will notify others when you are unavailable. This enables you to participate undisturbed in hobbies, interests and activities, managing your personal time and keeping you in balance regarding work, rest, and play.

3. **Agree a curfew time** both with work, family, and friends. Encourage your colleagues, team or organisation to agree, for example a 7pm to 7am curfew, with no expectation if you receive an email it will be answered, or a phone call will be responded to (unless you are on call out/shift working, etc.) Most business environments do not require 24/7 responses! Adopting a curfew

agreement safeguards everyone's health and well-being, helping people switch off and refresh before starting another work day. The repeat offender who sends out emails at 9pm will learn to accept no response is coming until tomorrow. Though I recognise that for some, working evenings may be a better option, the important factor is to set boundaries around expectations. Similarly, ensure family and friends know the time in the evening when you prefer not to respond to texts and calls. I grew up with the Golden Rule that past 10pm you did not ring people!

4.   **Create a healthy 'work' rhythm,** monitoring the number of working hours and taking regular breaks, particularly when working from home (which includes full-time parents or carers and those who are retired or currently not working). You will be more productive if you get some fresh air at lunchtime or take a coffee break. Such checks and balances mean you are less likely to feel exhausted due to screen fatigue or be worn out because you have not stopped all day. When you are over-tired you are more likely to be grumpy and/or uncommunicative with loved ones!

5.   **When working from home, close your office space at the end of office hours.** If you have a separate work room, shut the door. If your workspace is multifunctional, put your laptop and paperwork away to avoid being drawn back during the evening or over the weekend. If you have a separate work phone, leave it on your desk or in your work bag. Build in some down time to help transition from work mode to home mode e.g. exercise, go for a walk, relax to some music, even if this is just for 15 minutes.

6.   **Leave your laptop and work phone at home when you go on holiday** because the world of work can survive without you! If you have a phone for both work and home, be disciplined and don't read work emails. Your priority is to take a break, enjoy time with

those you are on holiday with and recharge your batteries. You will be more productive on your return by doing this.

Social media and the internet can be both a blessing and a curse if you are not on your guard in how you use them. Not only can they absorb a huge chunk of time but they have the potential to be detrimental to your well-being as you get sucked into other people's 'perfect' lives. The comparison game can creep in, making you feel inadequate or smug neither of which are healthy for maintaining good relationships with others. Equally, isolating behind a screen stops you building healthy friendships with others – you substitute genuine, authentic relationships with those that are superficial, never sharing how you truly feel. It is easier to wear a mask when you are connecting online or via text because your mood and behaviour are harder to read, even by a good friend or close work colleague. In person conversations have greater opportunity to challenge authenticity. By being genuine with each other stronger relationships are developed. If you feel the negative aspects of your emotional intelligence are activating more than usual, check your friendship circle. Are those you are connecting with energising or depleting you relationally? Do you feel weighed down by others' behaviour, their gossip, slander and negativity? Good friends support each other through difficult times. In contrast, it is good to 'unfriend' those who consistently deplete you emotionally.

Television, film and other media also have the power to shift your emotional well-being both positively and negatively. What you view feeds your mind, so make good choices. For example, if you find the doom and gloom of the news drags you down, restrict not only how often you take a look but the time of day you view e.g. avoid watching just before you go to bed. If you find certain types of films leave you feeling fearful and anxious, stop watching them!

Activity: Overcoming busyness

Which approval strategies have I adopted that affect how busy I allow myself to become? (People Pleaser, Saviour, Striver, Procrastinator, Perfectionist)

How recently have I experienced the Wheel of Reaction? What are/were my expectations and who can I talk to, to get off it and stay off it?

Which external drivers do I recognise and what changes can I make to help keep emotionally balanced?

Chapter 14. Personal resilience and coping with change

—

Managing emotional intelligence includes regularly reviewing how you remain productive and positive when faced with pressure and stress, uncertainty, and change. Your personal resilience can fluctuate, so it is important to recognise any shifts and catch yourself before it drops too far.

Resilience is being able to bounce back from setbacks and to keep going in the face of tough demands and difficult circumstances, including the enduring strength that builds from coping well with challenging or stressful events.[7]

The following five indicators will help you identify how stressed you are feeling and how effectively you are managing your personal resilience. Regularly reviewing your scores against each indicator enables you to quickly recognise when your resilience is moving downwards and, equally, to celebrate when it improves. Be aware of any incremental shift so that you can immediately put strategies in place to prevent your scores going any lower. The next chapter has many practical suggestions to help you keep balanced and manage your personal resilience.

Five indicators for managing pressure and stress

The scoring system for each of the five indicators is simple to follow and helps you identify where you are doing well and where you are struggling:

1–4   I recognise I am struggling and need to take immediate action to improve my score.

5–7   Doing OK but would be good to improve my score.

8–10   Feeling positive and in a good place.

1. **Flexibility** measures how you are managing changes in your life, both work and home and how easily you are able to adapt from Plan A to Plan B. Are you able to respond quickly and creatively to changes or do you find yourself rigid and resistant to any change that is required?

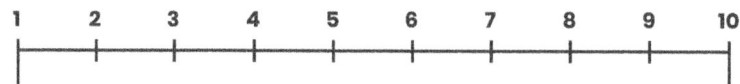

I find myself resisting change and being too rigid

I am quickly able to adapt to any changes

2. **Support** measures your support network, both at work and in your personal life. Do you have good support around you and feel able to ask for help? Alternatively, do you find yourself feeling isolated and unable to ask for help because you do not have anyone to turn to or you feel uncomfortable asking?

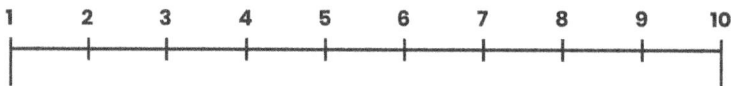

I am not asking for help and support and feel isolated

I have good support around me and access it when required

3. **Balance** measures whether your life feels in balance between work and your personal life, enabling you to enjoy and feel fulfilled in both.

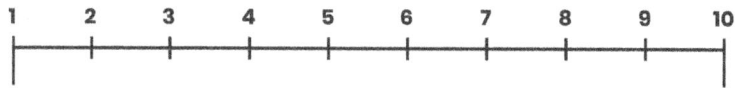

I feel out of control and am losing work–life balance

I am maintaining good work–life balance

4. **Goals** measures whether life has a sense of purpose and meaning:
    dreams, plans or goals you have set yourself to look forward to.
    Do you have momentum in your life or does it feel pointless with
    little or nothing to look forward to? It is OK to adapt or change
    goals due to your situation and circumstance but always have
    them, short-term and long-term, big and small.

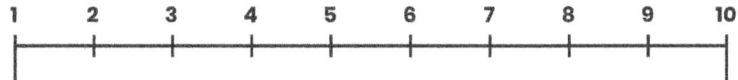

I have lost sight of goals
(personal or work) and life
feels lacking in purpose

I have clear goals and a
sense of purpose in life

5. **Emotional management** measures how your emotions are
    impacting on your life. Do you feel emotionally strong and in
    control of your responses to people and situations, with good
    self-belief and confidence? In contrast, are you emotionally out
    of control, angry one minute and tearful the next, with Prompts
    uncontrollably activating and affecting your confidence and self-
    belief?

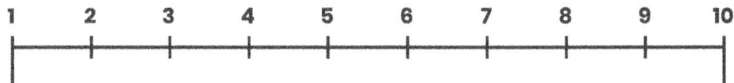

My emotions feel out of control/
up and down. My confidence and
self-belief are low

I have good emotional control
and strong confidence and
self-belief

If your scores are all between 8 and 10 that is great and keep
monitoring to ensure they stay at this level.

If some of your scores are between 5 and 7 take some time to review
what incremental step(s) you can take to build each of those up. If you
have more than two in the range 5–7, who can you chat to for help

and encouragement? The phrase, 'A problem shared ...' is true; family, friends and/or work colleagues can encourage you to make and stick to changes you choose that will build up your personal resilience.

If some of your scores are between 1 and 4, particularly in two areas or more, I encourage you to seek support from trusted friends, your family or work colleagues. There is no shame in asking for help and support which will enable you to rebuild your personal resilience. Choosing carefully who you share with also gives others the opportunity to come closer to you, building stronger relationships with those you reach out to. Please do not suffer in silence!

Activity: Maintaining personal resilience

Get into the habit of asking yourself these questions.

1. How am I doing against each of the five indicators?
2. What simple, practical steps can I take to increase the lower scores?
3. What steps can I take to maintain the higher scores?

Coping with change

Managing your personal resilience becomes particularly challenging in periods of major change and trauma. In your lifetime you may experience the loss of loved ones or other significant challenges in your personal circumstances, for example divorce or career paths. At some point you will experience a loss and the diagram below illustrates how to navigate and ultimately embrace such a change in your life.

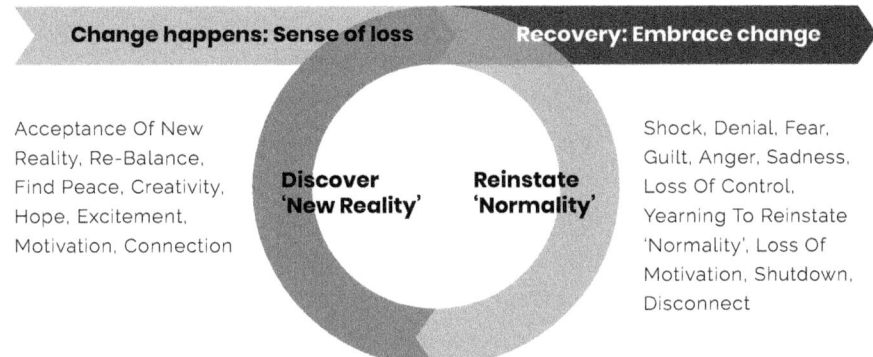

Change happens: Sense of loss | Recovery: Embrace change

Acceptance Of New Reality, Re-Balance, Find Peace, Creativity, Hope, Excitement, Motivation, Connection

Discover 'New Reality'

Reinstate 'Normality'

Shock, Denial, Fear, Guilt, Anger, Sadness, Loss Of Control, Yearning To Reinstate 'Normality', Loss Of Motivation, Shutdown, Disconnect

It can be helpful to work through any significant change or trauma by recognising what happens emotionally under extreme circumstances and work through these three stages of transition.

Stage 1 Shock

When significant change or trauma occurs, the natural response is to go into emergency mode and seek safety by shutting down and withdrawing into yourself. From an emotional point of view, it can feel like you are holding your breath until it feels safe to breath freely again. You may feel totally numb, exhausted and in denial with no capacity to try and make sense of what is happening or the motivation to do anything at all. You can feel total disconnection from yourself and the world around you, like being in a vacuum. In this initial stage it is important to acknowledge you will not be your 'best self'. Alongside a feeling of numbness, Prompts may be activating and emotions running high, not just shock, fear and panic but also sadness as you deny what is happening. You may feel anger at the loss of control and a compulsion to fight back as you yearn to reinstate 'normality'. The absolute priority is to be kind to yourself and not try to start processing it or 'pull yourself together' to support others when you have no capacity to do this. Realising you are in emergency mode and putting in place a care plan, which may simply be to allow others to help you and those you are responsible for, will give you the time and space before moving forward to the next stage.

Stage 2 Processing

Only when you come out of the initial shock will your rational mind begin to kick in, enabling you to practically process what is happening alongside 'feeling your feel'. The temptation is to either try too hard to push through that processing or use default coping methods in order to 'get back to normal'. Rather than overwhelming yourself with intense processing and so shutting down how you feel altogether, allow yourself time and space to bat around what you are processing both intellectually and emotionally. Your current trauma can also lift the lid on previous situations that you have experienced. At this stage, or when the time feels right, it can be helpful to talk things through with trusted family and friends or with professionals who are trained in supporting people through trauma.

Stage 3 Consolidation

Having given yourself time and space to process the change, you will find it easier to move towards consolidation and closure. This may involve going through the process of forgiveness covered in Chapter 12 and/or making the choice to move on. As you begin to feel greater acceptance of a 'new reality' – that things are different but you can move forward – you begin to breath normally and, as you re-balance, an improved sense of well-being emerges. Acceptance increases your motivation and hope begins to return. Such times of change enable you to recognise how you have grown through the experience enabling you to feel excitement about the new beginning. Connection with people becomes easier and recovery continues as the change is embraced.

The following chapter will provide you with many practical ways to help improve and maintain your personal resilience and support the recovery from major change and trauma.

Chapter 15. Maintaining balance

—

Prompts are most likely to be triggered when you are tired, stressed, feeling pressured, unwell or generally out of sync with life. To reduce these factors and experience greater contentment, it is important to build your personal resilience by creating greater balance in your life. You can achieve this using the following suggestions in your daily routine.

Gratitude. List and celebrate what you are grateful for every day to cultivate a 'heart of gratitude' for all that is good in your life, even when you face difficult times. It is so easy to focus on the negative and then miss the abundance that is all around you, which would help you feel better. A beautiful sunny day, support from a work colleague, the robin singing to you on the fence, your favourite cup of coffee, the laughter of a child, a warm bed to sleep  in. The list is endless if only you take the time to notice! Learn to capture these snapshots throughout your day; even take photos to look back on before you go to sleep, if that helps. Gratitude feeds contentment and suddenly each day feels better even in the most challenging of times.

Successes. List and celebrate daily successes: planned, unplanned (which have reshaped your day), big achievements and simple things. Share these with others. Congratulate yourself. Every day will have accomplishments, whether making a meal you enjoyed or completing a project or task. Celebrate your successes even if it is something as simple as getting out of bed and having a shower.

Avoid 'I should' lists. Be realistic with your 'to do' list, rather than setting yourself up to fail with an 'I should do this, I should do that'. You will end up going to bed feeling fed up because you have underachieved. Prioritise what is urgent and important (rocks and some pebbles) and the rest can wait!

Learn when to say 'No' rather than over-allowing with others. Identify why you struggle to say 'No'. Does it come from your learnt approval strategies and Prompts, for example a desire to please others and not let them down? Is it about what others will think of you or a fear of any repercussions if you refuse? Manage your emotional intelligence and change your beliefs to positive ones that enable you to say 'No'. Learn how to be firm but kind and 'say no with flowers', for example 'Regarding your deadline, I will struggle to meet that, but I could prepare it by ...'. If you literally struggle to hear the word 'No' come out of your mouth, practise saying and shouting it in the shower! Yes, I know this sounds crazy, but as you learn to do this it will become easier to say when an opportunity arises.

Choose not to turn on the landing lights for negative thoughts and beliefs to land. Instead, manage your internal narrative and stop believing your own negative publicity! Use 'Request Denied' to fend off any negative thoughts and learn to laugh at them so they have no hold over you. Focus on positive truths, for example 'I do belong here', 'I can do this', 'I am good enough/loved'.

Learn to be honest and authentic with your thoughts and feelings, safely processing any that are having a negative impact so that you can move forwards. When you recognise negative thoughts, it is important to reward yourself for having realised they are present. This is a positive achievement because what you are aware of, you can do something about! Having let go of some of the thoughts, beliefs and emotions (using the Trace the Triggers form on page 50) consider these next two questions to change the way you react in future situations:

1.   What can I do to bring more balance to the situation and myself?
2.   How will I choose to move forward, in this situation or one like it in the future, considering what I have learnt?

Do not wear 'masks' around others. Masks push people away whereas being yourself with people enables them to come closer. Build authentic, face-to-face relationships with others so you get to know them and vice versa.

Accept and absorb affirmation. When people acknowledge you, absorb it, breath it in and say, 'thank you'. By allowing yourself to receive compliments and thanks it not only builds your confidence and self-worth, but it also acknowledges and honours the individual who has complimented you.

Do not compare yourself to others. Think about an athlete running a 100m race and how they fix their eyes ahead towards the finish line. If they look across at others they run slower and, at worst, trip themselves up. You are not your sibling, your friend or work colleague, you are you! Instead of getting caught up in the comparison game, enjoy running in your own lane celebrating your uniqueness, skills, and talents.

Superior and inferior comparison are both unhealthy because they lead to either pride and smugness or discouragement and a sense of unworthiness – neither help build healthy relationships. Be aware of how you handle others' successes or failures and demonstrate respect and humility to them!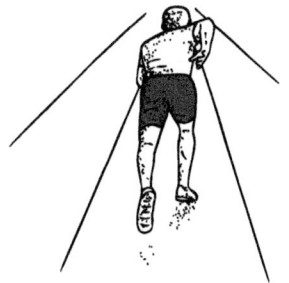

Do not judge others. When you have an issue with an individual, go to that person and seek to understand their perspective. Whilst managing 'your stuff', share how you feel and work together to resolve the situation with the aim of reconciliation. (Handling conflict and the Communication Wheel are covered in more detail in Part 3.)

Cultivate kindness. Consider the way you think of and serve others. It is surprising how helping others makes you feel more positive about life and improves your sense of well-being.

Participate in life. How you participate in life will look and feel quite different to others around you; do not do the comparison game! A job that brings fulfilment, authentic friendships, stronger connection with family, hobbies and interests can all bring a sense of balance and joy, peace, and calm. Get the balance right for you so that you feel energised, rather than drained, by life.

Prioritise quiet time daily and learn to 'Be still'. You are a Human BEING not a Human DOING. Contemplation, prayer or reflection can help build stillness in your day.

Plan rest time each week. Your body is not designed to work 24/7. Enjoy quality time with family and friends but also make time for yourself. An overload of social activity and connection with others, often the pitfall for extroverts, can lead to burn-out. If you are more introverted, recognise your need for quiet 'time out' to recharge.

Manage your use of social media and technology. It is easy to allow such tools to take over, which can lead to a sense of loneliness and isolation, existing in a world that is unreal. They are traps for the comparison game and distractions from building face-to-face relationships that enhance well-being.

Consider what you eat and drink, your sleep and exercise patterns. Your body requires the right fuel and rest to function effectively and efficiently.

Plan and take your full holiday entitlement. Spread it throughout the year and use the time to refresh. Leave your laptop or work mobile at home because the world of work can carry on without you.

Set and write down goals and dream big. It is great fun seeing dreams fulfilled: places you would like to visit, activities you want to experience, things you want to learn, people you wish to meet, etc.

Activity: Maintaining balance

Which of the suggestions for re-balancing can you particularly relate to and how do they link to your Prompts?

What steps can you take to bring greater daily balance?

Summary

—

Let us reflect on what you have covered in Part 2:

- Once you understand what is stored in your belief system, you can begin to redefine The Gap, shifting from negative to positive beliefs and thought patterns.

- There is a direct link between your inner thinking (deep roots, inner beliefs, vows) and how you outwardly behave. Drawing your Belief Tree helps you to understand the correlation between the two.

- Emotions aren't right or wrong, but how you express them can have a positive or negative impact. It is important to understand how to connect with and manage all your emotions.

- To build trust in any relationship requires you to forgive others, past or present; in that way you are not held captive to any hurts that affect current situations.

- Keeping your emotional intelligence in check includes being aware of how you prioritise time and not subscribing to unnecessary busyness.

- There are five indicators to help you maintain personal resilience: flexibility, support, balance, goals, emotional management. Regularly assessing your score for each helps you keep balanced so that responses to people and situations remain healthy and strong.

- When facing major change and trauma, be kind to yourself and allow time and space to work through its three stages: shock, processing, consolidation.

- Negative responses are most like to be triggered when you are tired, stressed, unwell or otherwise out of balance. Intentionally taking action to keep balanced enables you to experience greater enjoyment and contentment in life.

Part 3

Emotional intelligence and how you communicate, influence and lead

—

Chapter 16. Handling 'difficult' people and situations

—

Emotional intelligence is not just about self. 'My stuff' affects 'your stuff' and vice versa. There are commonalities between our own and other people's emotional intelligence in how we communicate, influence, and lead each other. I have a heartfelt belief most people do not get up in the morning with a conscious choice to be unkind or difficult. Things happen and people react, sometimes to the detriment of themselves and those they encounter. Whilst you are not responsible for others' emotional intelligence, by understanding and managing your own you are better equipped to handle people and situations, however difficult, more positively.

Day-to-day emotional mismanagement puts us on a potential collision course with others. Conflict will happen as soon as your 'concerns' appear to be incompatible with someone else's. A concern can be anything from a difference of opinion, priority, approach, idea, solution or plan. Whilst the list is endless, common themes in the cause of conflict are ambiguity and lack of clarity. What is important in any potential conflict situation is to 'stay in your adult place' by maturely managing your emotional intelligence so that trust is maintained or even enhanced, rather than broken. Creating trust takes time but can be damaged in an instant. I illustrate this by taking a piece of paper and ripping it in two. If you try to stick together the original sheet of paper, the tear will remain visible. Having broken trust, it is hard to rebuild and requires emotional maturity. Reconciliation will be far more effective if you talk everything through with the aim of respectfully resolving any differences. This includes making a choice to apologise and forgive when required, to agree not to bring up past demeanours again and start with a fresh piece of paper.

Conflict can easily escalate if you do not move to resolve an issue as it arises. Something happens, A blames B and B reacts to A and so on. Instead of communicating with the aim of openly discussing and resolving the issue, the temptation is to continue to blame others and ally yourself with those who will agree with you, which builds antagonism. Those involved begin to invest in the conflict creating a winner/loser mindset of 'open warfare'. Any past misdemeanours easily come into play: you believe something to be this way, you look for evidence, find it, build a case and this becomes your view of reality. This is when an attitude of hostility and hate can become entrenched, affecting relationships whether at work or in your personal life. Such an approach is a terrible waste of time and damaging to all those concerned, individually and collectively, directly and indirectly.

Client P contacted me to ask if I might support two teams reporting to him who had become dysfunctional and suspicious of each other following a merger of two organisations. The two teams were required to work closely together but there was an 'us and them' mindset. Mistrust was tangible, with little understanding or empathy for how the other team might be feeling or seeing things differently. Working initially with each of the teams and using picture postcards to visualise how individuals were feeling (there were a lot of Prompts being triggered in the room!), we were able to discuss how Team B felt threatened and undermined by Team A, who represented the 'takeover' organisation. The processes and procedures used for years were being challenged but the underlying fear was that they might lose their jobs. Team A were concerned that Team B's current processes and procedures would not align with their operation; they were keen to integrate systems because that would ultimately make everyone's life easier. Team A was reacting against what they perceived as a lack of co-operation when they were trying to help, which was being perceived by Team B as control and being told they were not good enough by Team A. Using the selected postcards to share how everyone was feeling and people's concerns, we were able to work towards a better understanding and an agreed plan of action. 'Buddying' relationships were set up to get to know each other, which led to improved understanding around tasks and activities as well as knowledge sharing between the two teams.

Failure to address even minor concerns and issues is rather like brushing dirt under a carpet. Eventually the mound will become large enough to trip you and others up and has the potential to be damaging. Instead of taking the time to get to know the individual and understand their perspective by putting yourself in their shoes, the easier option is simply to label someone as 'difficult'. When I ask the question 'What is a difficult colleague?' (also applies to family member, friend, etc.), those attending a workshop will enthusiastically give me an impressive list:

A difficult person is:
1.   Rude, aggressive, argumentative, impatient, stubborn.
2.   Consistently cynical, negative and pessimistic.
3.   Dishonest.
4.   Superior, disdainful stance.
5.   Over controls. Insular approach, not taking others' opinions into consideration. Does not listen/has their own agenda.
6.   Unrealistic expectations/their agenda.
7.   Does not respect decisions, thinks their opinion is right, goes behind your back.
8.   Not a team player: unsupportive, will not collaborate or participate, not share common goals, tramples over others' feelings/suggestions.
9.   Consumed with zooming in to see the detail rather than being able to zoom out to see the bigger picture (and vice versa).
10.   Overly compliant or silent – agrees or goes along with whatever others say instead of genuinely engaging and expressing their point of view.
11.   Overly dependent on others, not taking responsibility to develop or apply the knowledge or skills they need or have but use others to spoonfeed them answers or makes decisions for them.

12. Poor work ethic: unreliable, does not deliver, lazy, lack of care in what they deliver, ownership of mistakes (blame others).
13. Disorganised and last minute or late.
14. Inflexible, rigid, will not adapt to change.
15. Ambiguous, poor communicator.
16. Panicky, indecisive leadership.

Turning the question around, I then ask 'When have you been a difficult colleague? Was the label justified and what would have prevented you being, or being perceived as, difficult?' There is a moment when the penny drops and reality kicks in: that we can all be perceived as difficult on a regular basis! **If you point your finger at someone (the blame game) recognise three fingers point back at you!**

This raises the question 'What is my part in the situation and how can I resolve it constructively?' Self-awareness and self-management enable social awareness and relationship management. By managing your thoughts, feelings and beliefs you are more likely to handle such situations effectively. It is all too easy to play victim, that bad things always happen to you. But when you play this role your perspective and responses follow a negative pattern, making excuses, blaming others, saying you did not know and using language such as 'I can't', always waiting in the hope someone else will fix the situation. Rather than play the victim, manage 'your stuff' so that you can deal with the issue in a way that respects and honours others (the Trace the Triggers form will help). Be accountable for your actions, by taking the following positive steps:

1. Acknowledge the reality – practically and emotionally.
2. Own it – your role in it, apologise and forgive.
3. Find a solution.
4. Make it happen.

Confronting is a proactive action that helps to keep relationships functioning. In any confrontational situation it is not always easy to understand why you and the other party are upset or unhappy because you are both picking up not just words but non-verbal messages you do not understand or know how to handle. Seek to understand the 'mood music' in the room. Ask yourself 'What is more important, proving I am right or maintaining the relationship?' Work to achieve win–win by not being judgemental, attacking and dominant or acting as a victim. Instead, remain equal in the situation and demonstrate emotional maturity by knowing your Prompts and insecurities and how you respond to stress, i.e. do not let your thoughts, feelings and beliefs rule you. Consider the other person's threat response by recognising they are showing flight (retreat) or fight (attack/active or passive aggression) behaviour and consider their possible Prompts based on what they are sharing (verbally and non-verbally). Demonstrate you care by giving your complete attention, asking good questions, actively listening and demonstrating a curiosity to understand. Be aware of your non-verbal signals, for example maintaining eye contact, nods and smiles and not looking at your phone or computer, when you need to give your full attention to the individual. Empathise through connecting verbally and non-verbally before you respond. Be prepared to show a level of authenticity and vulnerability to resolve the issue together.

Speech has the potential to be one of the most powerful weapons available to humans. Its power can either encourage and build up an individual or put down and destroy them. The 'triple filter' test is accredited to the great Greek philosopher, Socrates. Many consider it a great life lesson that can help deal with gossip and rumours. The anecdote is that someone offered Socrates unsolicited information about a friend but before they could continue he asked, 'If what you want to tell me isn't true, isn't good and isn't even useful, why would I want to hear it?' Before speaking consider the three filters:

Filter 1 truthfulness: Is what I am about to say true? Have I got all the facts and are they accurate or are they based on hearsay or others' perceptions?

Filter 2 usefulness: Is what I am about to say or do necessary? Is there a purpose?

Filter 3 goodness: Is what I am about to say or do kind?

It is important to challenge when you feel it necessary but do so in a way that addresses the issue rather than attacking the character of an individual. I like to express this through the phrase 'Say it with flowers', for example 'If you would like my help looking through any future reports, please feel free to ask' rather than 'If you had asked, I would have helped you'.

Managing 'your stuff' and picking up and responding effectively to any signal others are communicating, can make the difference between resolving an issue successfully and having to live under a cloud of negativity and unresolved issues. Be known as someone who builds strong relationships through being truthful, purposeful, empathetic and kind.

Activity: How I handle difficult people and situations

From the 'difficult person' (friend, family member) list, what can you relate to in respect of how others may see you?

How do these behaviours link to your emotional intelligence, i.e. what Prompts are easily triggered?

How do you choose to move forward in the way you handle 'conflict' situations?

Chapter 17. How to communicate and influence effectively

—

The basic elements for communication are quite simple. A message is sent to the receiver, which often results in the receiver sending a message back. However, what we see, hear, touch, taste and smell go through our emotional filters in how we see ourselves and the world around us. Filters that easily delete, distort and generalise the communication that has been sent and received.

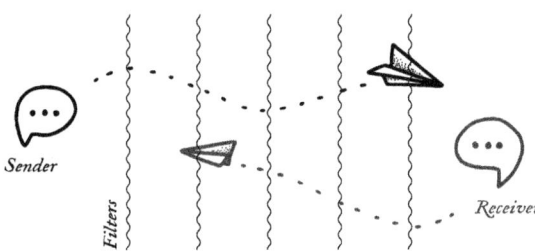

We have an experience or observation and then add meaning. We make assumptions and draw our own conclusions. Such conclusions impact on what we believe and how we respond to any belief that has been activated. Consequently, communication is not as simple as it would appear; it is only as good as the perception of reality by the parties involved in any given moment, as it changes so easily and rapidly.

A strong relationship between two people involves both parties communicating any issue. Issues are different to problems because a problem represents difficulty. However, issues can become problems depending on how you react, or handle a given situation. When an issue is not handled effectively and keeps cropping up, the issue can then become a problem. Equally, an issue becomes a problem when it is not identified, or there is a refusal to deal with it. The ability to effectively communicate your issue is not always easy, often because of your emotionl intelligence and the barriers you put up when you communicate to others. Even the thought of having to have a 'difficult' conversation can easily activate your Prompts leading to a reaction. Whether with your partner, friend or work colleague, the fear of saying the wrong thing or being misunderstood can shut you down before you have even tried to resolve the issue. Unfortunately, such avoidance solves nothing. That difficult conversation must take place or you risk permanently harming a relationship.

Alongside the Trace the Triggers form, the Communication Wheel[8] provides a practical way to talk through issues and concerns safely with others, hopefully avoiding negative conflict and the breakdown of trust in a relationship. There is flexibility in how you use the Wheel and you do not always have to use every step.

The Communication (Awareness) Wheel

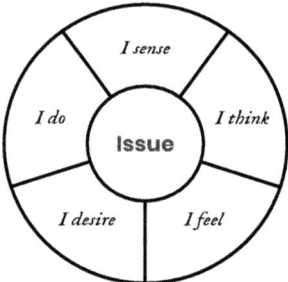

1. **Sensing** What am I seeing, hearing, sensing (touching, tasting, smelling)? Sensing does the same job that a good reporter does i.e. observes and describes the facts and examples, without any judgement or interpretation. There is a difference between sensations and interpretations and the danger is that you can state your opinions and interpretations as though they are facts.

2. **Thinking** What is my internal narrative saying to me about how I am interpreting what I heard or observed? What are my thoughts,

beliefs, ideas, interpretations, opinions, assumptions and judgements that have come into play?

3. **Feeling** How has the situation made me feel? What emotions have surfaced from the experience? Your feelings are the spontaneous responses to a situation and may conflict with each other. If your teenage child is late home, you may feel both angry and relieved. Recognise some people have a harder time understanding, identifying and expressing feelings than others – you may have been working on your emotional intelligence when they have not!

4. **Desire** What is it I want from myself or others in this situation? My intentions, aspirations, hopes, longings, goals? What can I do to resolve the situation or how would I handle a similar situation differently in the future? Intentions typically involve an attitude of moving towards or away from something, for example 'If I have said something that has upset you, tell me so that we can talk about it' (in this case recognise/accept that the individual may find it difficult to talk about it so be kind and patient).

5. **Action** What actions (plans, proposals, promises, behaviours (not opinions or attitudes), activities, accomplishments) are required to resolve the issue by myself to improve the situation now or in the future?

It is important to use 'I' statements when using the Communication Wheel because you can only know for sure what you have seen, heard, felt, wanted, etc. and can only speak for yourself. The habit of speaking for others by using 'You' statements is often learnt in childhood; it creates tension in the conversation because it points your finger at recipients of such statements and puts them on the defensive. 'I' statements are not intended to encourage self-centeredness or selfish attitudes but rather, to keep the responsibility for your thoughts and feelings on yourself.

Use the Trace the Triggers form and the Communication Wheel to reflect on an experience or situation before you communicate to others. Such an approach enables you to handle people and situations positively. Processing your Prompts honestly helps you to see the impact of 'your stuff'. As you analyse the situation, to enable you to deal with the issue objectively, remove any judgements and unkind thoughts that attack the character of others involved. Conflict happens when your version of the story or that of others involved replaces reality. It is the mood music in the room that controls reactive responses rather than talking through the issue with the aim of reconciliation. Pushing the pause button helps you to gain a new perspective and sometimes such reflection can eliminate the need to have a discussion because you have realised it is your Prompts that are being activated!

Client Q was upset that her boss had yet again changed his mind on something when she had already put a plan of action in place. She thought he was undermining her authority and being disrespectful and unfair, particularly because she had made the effort to sort the activities at the expense of spending time with her family. This made her feel angry, resentful, sad and guilty. She shared what she had sensed and the Prompts that had been triggered with her boss; he had no idea she felt this way because, as he then explained, in his mind they were still draft ideas not final decisions. He apologised for the misunderstanding and she apologised for reacting aggressively. My client suggested that in future it would help to discuss whether he was processing ideas or making a final decision so that she knew what was required of her. Both agreed to build clarity into any further discussions. Talking through the issue using the Communication Wheel helped them both understand each other better, their different perspectives and how best to work together, optimising each other's strengths as 'idea generator' alongside 'activator'.

Learn to pay attention to the other person's non-verbal communication rather than just what they say verbally. It is useful to remember that 93% of communication is non-verbal, so even when you feel you have said the right things your non-verbal signals and tone may say otherwise, and vice versa. Expert communicators are not only aware of what they say verbally and non-verbally, they are also active listeners, reading and responding to all the messages the other person is sending. They use verbal and non-verbal communication to indicate they are interested in what is shared e.g. nods of encouragement that they want to hear more. Such responses invite disclosure and help to create an atmosphere of reconciliation. Be honest and authentic, gracious and respectful, and take ownership of your part in any situation.

Activity: The Communication Wheel

Use the following as a template to help familiarise yourself with the five steps of the Communication Wheel.

Step 1 Sensing	What I am seeing, hearing, sensing (the facts)
Step 2 Thinking	My internal thoughts, beliefs, ideas, interpretations, opinions, assumptions, judgements.
Step 3 Feeling	How has the situation made me feel?

Step 4 Desire	What is it I want from myself or others in this situation? What are my intentions, aspirations, hopes, goals?
Step 5 Action	What plans, proposals, promises, behaviours activities are required to resolve the issue?

Effective influencing

Influencing is not about manipulation or misuse of power. Like communication, influencing is a daily skill used at work or in the home. Whether you are selling an idea, a plan or an approach, persuading others to see your point of view or convincing them your ideas will work requires you to manage your emotional intelligence to have an impact on the outcome.

Successful influencing is about combining the 'what' with the 'how'. The 'what' of influencing is task focused, based on your knowledge and experience. It is about presenting ideas logically and persuasively and truthfully, so that others can understand and appreciate the value of your proposals. The 'how' of influencing is people focused, establishing and maintaining good relationships so that those you wish to influence are receptive to considering your suggestions.

My experience working with clients is that most focus on either the 'what' or the 'how', rather than recognising the importance of balancing both. The skills required vary from the ability to plan and organise (what, where, why, how, and when) to being able to sell the benefits and defend the proposal by being clear about exactly what you want to achieve. Good communication skills, such as speaking, questioning, listening, summarising, using positive body language and the ability to build rapport, are equally important.

It is easy to fall into the trap of 'child to child' behaviour when your desire to influence does not go your way, like toddlers having a tantrum. Alternatively, we may resort to 'parent to child' command and control when we feel unable to influence an outcome. Learn how to 'stay in your adult place', managing your emotional intelligence as people seek to understand what you are communicating. Putting the relationship first and actively listening, you are more likely to get a positive result. Your ability to influence is, to a large extent, linked to the way people perceive you. If you are regarded as someone who is fair, reasonable and honest and who shows genuine concern for other people's feelings and points of view, people are more likely to listen to you. Equally, if you are perceived as arrogant, unreasonable, economical with the truth and showing little regard for other people's opinions and concerns, people will be unwilling to be influenced by you. To persuade people to hear and understand what you have to say it is important to actively listen to what they have to say. You can facilitate this by asking questions to find out their concerns. Your emotional intelligence will be on display non-verbally for everybody to read, so use open and friendly body language to communicate, alongside your words and your good intentions. Finally, pitch what you are proposing at the right level, not condescending or patronising and not too technical or jargon-filled as this will immediately switch people off and/or activate their Prompts, which could generate a negative response.

To encourage others to agree and act, recognise people are motivated to raise objections and push back for several reasons:

1. **Misunderstanding**, because you have not been clear in what you communicated. Equally, the other person may have spotted a legitimate issue with what is being suggested that needs to be adjusted or reconsidered.

2. **Misalignment** with the vision that is driving the change. The aimed-for outcome clashes with their values or preferences.

3. **Fear**, often associated with fear of unpredictability, failure and rejection. For example, 'If I can't adapt to new processes and procedures, I'll lose my job'.

4. **Impossibility**, that the change required of them cannot be achieved. For example, they are expected to master new technology and cannot imagine themselves being able to learn this.

5. **Habit**, and a reluctance to change because, 'I have done it this way successfully for years, so why change?'

6. **Negative impacts** the change could have on their working lives. For example, having to do more, working longer/unsocial hours, more tedious, 'outside' their role. They do not feel equipped with the necessary knowledge, skills and resources therefore work will be more stressful.

By reading the 'mood music' in the room and what is being shared (verbally and non-verbally), identify which of these objections are affecting those you want to influence. **Seek to manage obstacles with dignity and respect.** For example, when dealing with fear give reassurance, using examples of when similar action worked and what support is available. If you are dealing with habit, emphasise the benefits they will enjoy when the plan goes ahead. Resistance usually comes from a feeling of 'It's easier to resist than change, stick to what I know.' If you recognise misunderstanding then reiterate your arguments simply, clearly, logically and empathetically, in a way that works for the individual or group. Answer the unspoken question, 'What's in it for me?' There will be times when the outcome quite simply is a worse deal for an individual, often because the greater good requires a change to happen. Put yourself in their shoes and show empathy in these situations alongside helping the person recognise things must change.

Your emotional intelligence and ability to communicate and influence others are interconnected. Effective communication and influencing require you to evaluate and manage your thoughts and emotions whilst managing the expectations, fears and concerns of others. Having a greater understanding of your emotional intelligence as well as developing your skills as a communicator and influencer, will enable you to build stronger relationships both at work and in your personal life.

Chapter 18. Leadership and emotional intelligence

—

What do you look for in a leader and how does your emotional intelligence impact on the way you lead or follow others? Whether you are in a formal leadership role or part of various teams, your life will be affected by the leadership you provide and experience daily. When a leader lacks self-awareness and fails to manage 'their stuff', teams suffer, are unable to perform at their best and, at worst, become dysfunctional.

Leadership vs management

Leadership differs from management. Management is 'the skill or practice of controlling, directing or planning something'.[9] There will be daily management responsibilities: running a home, organising a classroom, managing an office or ensuring the smooth running of a business, hospital ward or department in a shop, etc. Management is the world of doing! Leadership looks and feels different; it is visionary and is about the projection of personality and character to inspire a group of people to achieve an agreed outcome. A successful leader is someone who understands themselves, the environment in which they operate and the people they are privileged to lead; seeing leadership in this way often causes a few comments when I facilitate groups of leaders. Imagine how different the world would be if all leaders saw leadership as a privilege across all areas of society, however tough they find their team, their situation and the future. As a leader, ask yourself 'Is my team there to serve me or am I there to serve them?' A provoking question indeed! Often the challenges of management take over but it is important to learn how to balance everyday activities with being a good leader to developing healthier, happier and ultimately more productive people.

Leadership in the 21st century

Over the past 40 years the world of work and pace of life has changed significantly. Job security has been replaced with a sense of career stability that comes from effectively managing your own path. This has led to a more individualistic approach, with people travelling like hitchhikers between different roles and organisations, moving on when the time feels right. Alternatively, they are forced to leave due to redundancy or changes to structures and roles that do not meet their expectations.

As well as a more mobile workforce there is a much higher emphasis on profit, performance and efficiency with an expectation to deliver because this is seen as the way for an organisation to survive against competition. The world of work has become transactional at the expense of investing in relationships (with employees, customers, suppliers, etc.) that are the heart of the organisation. In a climate of increasing competition, the emphasis becomes more and more about performance, efficiency and profit; organisations can easily drift away from the original vision and design that inspired many a founder in the first place. It is the culture of targets, deliverables, compliance and regulation that creates a mix of fear and anxiety about not delivering what is expected. Directors and other senior leaders, who are under constant pressure to raise standards, must also find efficiency savings and hit targets to satisfy key stakeholders. To achieve this, compounded by time constraints and lack of leadership development, they can fall into the trap of focusing on managerial delivery rather than being the inspiring, encouraging, respectful leaders people seek. Of course, not all companies operate under the 'purely for profit' model and it is encouraging to learn about new studies that highlight the future of successful business being a combination of profit and purpose, with a new dialogue taking place on the role of business in society today[10].

Unhealthy leadership styles

Over the years I have coached many wonderful people navigating the pathway of corporate success, across all levels of leadership. What I have discovered is that it is easy to fall foul of one or more unhealthy leadership styles, which negatively impacts on the leader, their team(s) and their families. Whether you are in a formal leadership role or come under someone else's leadership, some or all the unhealthy leadership styles listed below may be familiar to you.

Performance-driven. Focused on targets, standards, systems and procedures, interested in results and undertaking activities – both at work and at home. People are left feeling ignored, undervalued and demotivated because of the need to meet impossibly high standards .

Controller. Refuses to delegate because things are better done their way, often with a sense of 'I know best'. Keeps everything close to ensure all is undertaken 'correctly' to stay on top. No decisions can be made without their input and approval. People around hold back, operating from a place of compliance or fear of saying or doing the wrong thing. As a result, innovation and creativity suffer. The corrosive effect of 'ego' destroys the potential for any self-directed team. This behaviour continues at home or, due to the pressure of work, the home decisions are abdicated to someone else.

Overtime fanatic. Works all hours to ensure work is completed and targets met. Weekends and evenings exist to catch up so that the boss thinks they are a good performer. Emails fly out around the clock, particularly Sunday evening, with the expectation that others will show equal dedication because that is the way to succeed. Home life fits around the schedule of work.

Always available. Phone and laptop on tap all the time, including weekends and when on holiday. Believes the world cannot survive without their input; everyone can be contacted at any one time so that makes it OK. Constant availability means everyone is reassured. There are no boundaries between home and work and relationships suffer.

People pleaser. Over-accommodates and tries to look after everyone despite pressure to hit deadlines. When everyone goes home, tackles their work even if it means long hours and not being there for family and friends. It is exhausting and often leads to burn-out.

If you identify with any of these unhealthy leadership styles, recognise the underlying symptoms are rooted in your emotional intelligence and the voice you listen to in your head – your negative internal voice and lies you are believing about yourself and the world around you.

Activity: Unrelenting standards

Take a minute to ask yourself the following questions. (You may identify a behaviour/belief here that needs adding to your Belief Tree!)

Standard	Yes/No

Do I need to be the best at most things I do?

Am I unable to settle for 'good enough'?

Do I feel constant pressure to achieve?

Do I hate not winning?

Do I have a strong need to meet my responsibilities?

Do I need to be liked to feel valued?

Do I seek attention to prove my worth?

It is important to acknowledge when you are setting yourself unrelenting standards alongside the need to feel valued and loved. Such standards simply feed your fear of failure, fear of rejection (demotion, redundancy, disciplinary), self-reliance (i.e. pride), control, judgements and unforgivingness towards others. When leaders operate from such standards, the effects of their negative thought patterns cascade down from senior director level, through middle management and onwards to the frontline workforce. As a 'follower' you can easily buy into unhelpful beliefs when working under such leadership styles, reflecting back to the leaders what they are projecting:

1.   If I fail to meet targets, I will lose my job and/or status.
2.   Getting something wrong will reflect badly and weaken my position for promotion and job retention.
3.   To ensure the task is done correctly I will have to do it myself.
4.   Trust no one and watch your back.
5.   Play the game and say what needs to be said, do what is expected – do not rock the boat.
6.   If everyone is pleased with me then my position is safe.

Remember that putting yourself under this stress can leak into your personal life in terms of how you are feeling and behaving. In a different way, this can become the underpinning structure of your relationship with family and friends, it doesn't just happen at work. An unrelenting parent placing high expectations on a child's performance contributes to the evidence being stored in that child's belief system. For example, 'Love is conditional on performance' creates fear of rejection and 'Failure is not an option' leads to fear of failure.

As these unhelpful beliefs bounce between the leader and the followers they entrench, activating everyone's Prompts along the way and becoming the way things are done, while whether they are healthy is not being questioned. Sadly, such leadership behaviour makes for unhappy followers, unhappy families and, if we are honest, unfulfilled and unhappy leaders. By understanding and managing your emotional intelligence you are better positioned to demonstrate healthier leadership, whether in a formal role or simply the way you conduct yourself around others. Be aware when you are emotionally activated and therefore displaying unhealthy leader or follower behaviours and choose to respond positively. Learn to anticipate, avoid, and mitigate their impact. Seek to powerfully display something different and more positive to those around you, whether you are a leader or a follower.

Client R made the decision to influence the culture of the team he worked in. Instead of reacting emotionally to the negative behaviours and culture around him, which were unpleasant due to gossip, slander and people just not caring for one another, he began to look for small ways to show kindness and consideration. He would take in cakes, make drinks for everyone and intentionally help or take time to listen to colleagues. Gradually others began to follow his lead and the culture started to improve. After several months, his manager called him into his office and shared how he had noticed the difference in the way the team was interacting and thanked him for what he had done. I love this story because it shows how one team member, by exercising emotional maturity, can lead by example and make a positive difference.

Leadership is a reciprocal relationship between those who choose to lead and those who decide to follow. Even those who have a formal leadership title face the reality that if no one follows, they are simply taking a solitary walk on their own. It is a horrible thing to look over your shoulder only to discover nobody there but this can easily happen when people are forced to follow through compliance, rather than choosing to follow out of commitment to the leader! This raises an interesting question: what do followers look for in a leader that makes them choose to follow? I believe the following attributes in any leader attract followers:

- Provides vision and direction by being passionate and showing commitment to their vision.
- Shows enthusiasm and optimism.
- Demonstrates personal integrity.
- Practises what they preach.

- Develops other people, bringing out the best in them, focusing on the unique strengths of each.
- Recognises individual effort.
- Supports and actively listens to the ideas, challenges and worries of others. (They recognise they have two ears and one mouth, and use them in this proportion!)
- Encourages teamwork.
- Actively encourages feedback.
- Is accepting of change (but not change for change's sake).

The underpinning foundation of all these attributes is the ability of a leader to build empathy with others. **Despite us all living constantly with technology, business is about people!** Leaders who appreciate the reciprocal nature of leadership, demonstrate the importance and benefits of teamwork and are inclusive, not exclusive, inviting others to participate in their vision.

By empathising and choosing to work together collaboratively, healthier, stronger relationships are forged. The irony is that leaders who prioritise the relational aspect of leadership, caring for and serving their community rather than simply focusing on the 'doing' of management, build stronger, more productive and more committed teams. For this reason alone, relational leadership based on emotional maturity makes sense!

Activity: Leader and follower styles

Which of the unhealthy leader and/or follower styles do I recognise?

Which Prompts/Golden Rules/beliefs are activated alongside such styles? (Refer to your Belief Tree.)

What steps can I take to change my approach to people and situations?

Summary

—

Let us reflect on what you have covered in Part 3:

- Through understanding and managing your emotional intelligence, you are better equipped to communicate, influence and lead.

- An important part of emotional intelligence is the ability to show empathy, by taking the time to get to know others and understand their perspective, putting yourself in their shoes.

- Your thoughts, feelings and beliefs easily delete, distort, and generalise any communication sent and received. When communicating, apply the triple filter test: is what I am about to say based on truth, is there a purpose to sharing it, is it kind?

- 93% of communication is non-verbal so be aware of your non-verbal signals and tone of voice, which contribute to the 'mood music in the room'. Become an active listener, positively reading and responding to others' communication.

- The Communication Wheel provides a practical way to talk through issues and concerns safely with others: I sense, I think, I feel, I desire, I do.

- In any potential conflict situation 'stay in your adult place' by maturely managing your emotional intelligence so that trust is maintained or even enhanced, rather than broken.

- Recognise when you are or are being perceived as, a 'difficult colleague'. Remember, when you point the finger at someone three point back at you! Ask yourself, 'What's my part in this conflict situation?'

- Successful influencing is about the 'what' (task-focused, based on your knowledge, facts and experience) and the 'how' (people-focused). Your emotional intelligence plays a key role in establishing and maintaining good relationships so that others are receptive to your suggestions.

- Management is the world of stuff and doing. Leadership is visionary and the projection of personality and character to inspire a group of people to achieve their desired outcome. As a leader consider what you are projecting and the shadow you are casting over others.

- Leadership is a reciprocal relationship between those who choose to lead and those who decide to follow. Be aware when you are emotionally activated and therefore displaying an unhealthy leadership behaviour: performance-driven, controller, overtime fanatic, always available, people pleaser. Ask yourself, 'Am I a leader I would choose to follow?'

Keeping on track

—

As human beings we never stop learning. However, once we leave full-time education we tend to focus on our intellectual learning and consider our personal and leadership development less. This can prove problematic not only in our careers but also our personal relationships as we engage with the world around us. As a leadership coach I often encounter senior leaders and managers who have developed their professional skills and are highly competent technically, but their self-awareness and leadership skills are underdeveloped and this trips them up as they transition to roles that involve communicating, influencing, and leading others.

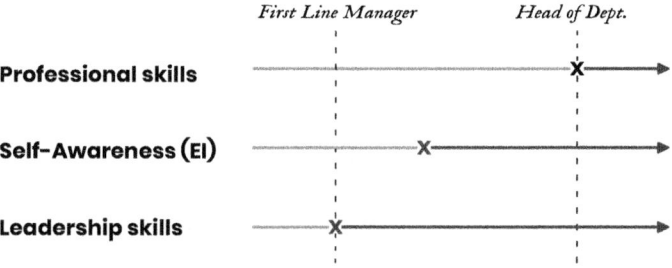

Understanding and managing your emotional intelligence alongside a toolkit of basic leadership skills are essential if you want to create and maintain stronger relationships with yourself and those around you. Learning to manage 'your stuff' and how it impacts on your responses to people and situations enables you to connect with others in a healthier, more meaningful way. Whether you are in a formal leadership role at work or lead in other ways e.g. your family, clubs and societies or voluntary work, recognise the 'children' are watching you. Whether literally your family, those that report to you at work or others you encounter daily, all observe your behaviour and how you lead. How you conduct yourself will affect what they learn from you and how they choose to interrelate with others in the future. For this reason, I encourage you to keep dipping into the contents of this book allowing yourself to peel back further layers of your emotional intelligence onion so that you continue to learn and grow. Recognise the opportunity to teach and be an example to others through your conduct and behaviour and the relationships you build around you.

Keeping on track: six practical steps

1. Use the Trace the Triggers form to understand and change the way you think about and react to challenging situations. The more you use that and recognise your patterns of behaviour, the more likely that you will be able to catch yourself and choose to respond positively.

2. Keep referencing and updating your Prompt list and Belief Trees (original and new) as a reminder not to buy in to your old, negative set-ups. Make the choice to live by your new beliefs from your positive tree.

3. Keep monitoring your personal resilience by regularly reviewing the five pressure indicators (flexibility, support, balance, goals, emotional management). Make incremental changes to ensure scores remain between 8 and 10, whatever challenges life throws at you.

4. Have fun with the strategies for keeping balanced and keep using them! Review regularly and put into practice those that help you find greater emotional balance and well-being. All are useful but some will be particularly relevant at different times.

5. Use the Communication Wheel and triple filter test to resolve issues as they arise and manage conflict situations with dignity and respect by managing 'your stuff' before it negatively affects others.

6. Though not for everyone, you may like to keep a journal – recording your successes, what you are grateful for, what you are doing differently, how you see/feel differently about yourself, others, a situation and your experiences. If this works for you, go for it!

My final thought is one that has greatly influenced me over many years, it is from Victor Frankl[11] one of the Jewish survivors from the Holocaust, **'The last of the human freedoms is to choose one's attitude in any given set of circumstances.'** This quote is a powerful reminder that we can make the choice to not allow any circumstances to control how we position ourselves. By making the choice to change your inner thinking you can discover the riches of the outer aspects of your world and in so doing, get more from your life.

Templates

—

1   **Trace the Triggers form**

2   **Belief tree**

3   **Communication Wheel**

Activity – Trace the Triggers form

What's happened? (The trigger)

What's the concern? (My Projection)

	What emotion do you feel? (Please tick the boxes)					
	Love / Joy	Sadness	Guilt / Shame	Anger / Disgust	Fear / Panic	
Thoughts about Myself						Prompt(s)
Thoughts about others						Prompt(s)

How did I react?

Result (my reflection on the outcome)

My Belief Tree

**Outward behaviour
(what others see/sense)**

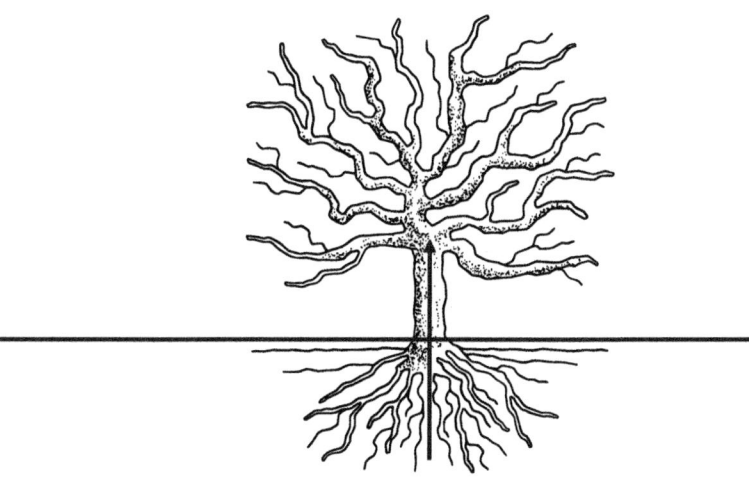

**Inner beliefs, vows and
judgements (unseen by others)**

The Communication Wheel

Step 1 Sensing	What I am seeing, hearing, sensing (the facts)
Step 2 Thinking	My internal thoughts, beliefs, ideas, interpretations, opinions, assumptions, judgements.
Step 3 Feeling	How has the situation made me feel?
Step 4 Desire	What is it I want from myself or others in this situation? What are my intentions, aspirations, hopes, goals?
Step 5 Action	What plans, proposals, promises, behaviours activities are required to resolve the issue?

Endnotes

—

1. The Big Five Personality Traits: The initial model was advanced by Ernest Tupes and Raymond Christal in 1961 but failed to reach an academic audience until the 1980s. In 1990, J.M. Digman advanced his five-factor model of personality, which Lewis Goldberg extended to the highest level of organisation. These five overarching domains have been found to contain and subsume most known personality traits and are assumed to represent the basic structure behind all personality traits. Peter Salovey and John Mayer in their 2004 'Emotional Intelligence. Theory, Findings ad Implications' Psychological Enquiry developed the 'ability' model.

2. Definition of EQ, EI and EIQ: Coleman A (2008) *A Dictionary of Psychology* (3ed.), Oxford University Press.

3. William James was an American philosopher, historian, and psychologist, and the first educator to offer a psychology course in the United States. James is considered to be a leading thinker of the late nineteenth century, one of the most influential philosophers of the United States and the 'Father of American psychology'.

4. Management trainer Martin M. Broadwell described the levels of competence as 'The Four Levels of Teaching' in February 1969. Paul R. Curtiss and Phillip W. Warren mentioned the model in their 1973 book *The Dynamics of Life Skills Coaching*. The model was used at Gordon Training International by its employee Noel Burch in the 1970s where it was called the 'four stages for learning any new skill'.

5. The Holy Bible (2011), Matthew (7:18), New International Version (Anglicised edition), Biblica (formerly International Bible Society).

6. Although the origins and history of many of the ideas and theories

associated with the Enneagram of personality are a matter of dispute, contemporary Enneagram theories are principally derived from the teachings of the Bolivian psycho-spiritual teacher Oscar Ichazo from the 1950s and the Chilean psychiatrist Claudio Naranjo from the 1970s. Naranjo's theories were also influenced by some earlier teachings about personality by George Gurdjieff and the Fourth Way tradition.

7. Cooper C., Flint-Taylor J. and Pearn C. (2013) *Building Resilience for Success: A Resource for Managers and Organizations*, ISBN 9780230361287

8. The Communication Wheel (Miller, Sherod & Phyllis) is a model consisting of The Awareness Wheel and Listening Cycle designed to improve communications in all kinds of relationships.

9. The Chambers Dictionary, 'Management', www.chambers.co.uk (accessed 25 October 2021).

10. https://www.cranfield.ac.uk/som/case-studies/coca-cola-enterprises-combining-profit-and-purpose.

11. Viktor Emil Frankl (1905–1997), an Austrian neuologist, philosopher, author and Holocaust survivor. He was the founder of logotherapy, which is underpinned by the tenet that searching for a life meaning is the central human motivational force.

Recommended reading
—

Emotional Intelligence and Working with Emotional Intelligence omnibus, by Daniel Goleman, outlines what emotional intelligence (EI) is all about and how it can be nurtured and strengthened in all of us. Goleman demonstrates that EI at work matters twice as much as cognitive abilities such as intellectual intelligence or technical expertise.

The New Leader, by Daniel Goleman, is a convincing description of the importance of emotional intelligence in leaders, arguing that it can be developed by working with EI coaches. Goleman gives a great business argument for developing it and how it can contribute to the bottom line.

Molecules of Emotions by Candace Pert covers the science behind emotions.

Feel the fear and do it anyway and *End of the struggle and dance with Life*, both by Susan Jeffers, are practical books that can bring insight around self-awareness and a more fulfilled lifestyle. Her books compliment teaching of emotional intelligence.

Battlefield of the Mind by Joyce Meyer explores how our actions are a direct result of our thoughts. If we have a negative mind, we will have a negative life.